A CONNECTING DOOR

A CONNECTING DOOR

Why we need to keep on asking questions and being asked questions

David Glessal Millar

International Psychoanalytic Books (IPBooks)
New York • http://www.IPBooks.net

A Connecting Door: Why We Need to Keep on Asking Questions and Being Asked Questions

Published by IPBooks, Queens, NY

Online at: www.IPBooks.net

ISBN: 978-1-956864-25-0

David Millar is a grammar schoolboy from Birmingham born in the middle of the war. He read chemistry at the University of Newcastle-upon-Tyne, theology at St Catharine's College, Cambridge and was Vicar of West Dean, Sussex.

Leaving the church in 1975, he read psychology at Birkbeck College London and trained as a clinical psychologist at the University of Leeds. He is a Lifetime Honorary Senior Clinician, Tavistock and Portman NHS Foundation Trust, where he was a Consultant Clinical Psychologist and Head of the Tavistock multidisciplinary adult psychoanalytic psychotherapy training. He is a Fellow, training and supervising analyst, and one-time Chair of Education of the British Psychoanalytical Society and Institute of Psychoanalysis.

Harborne

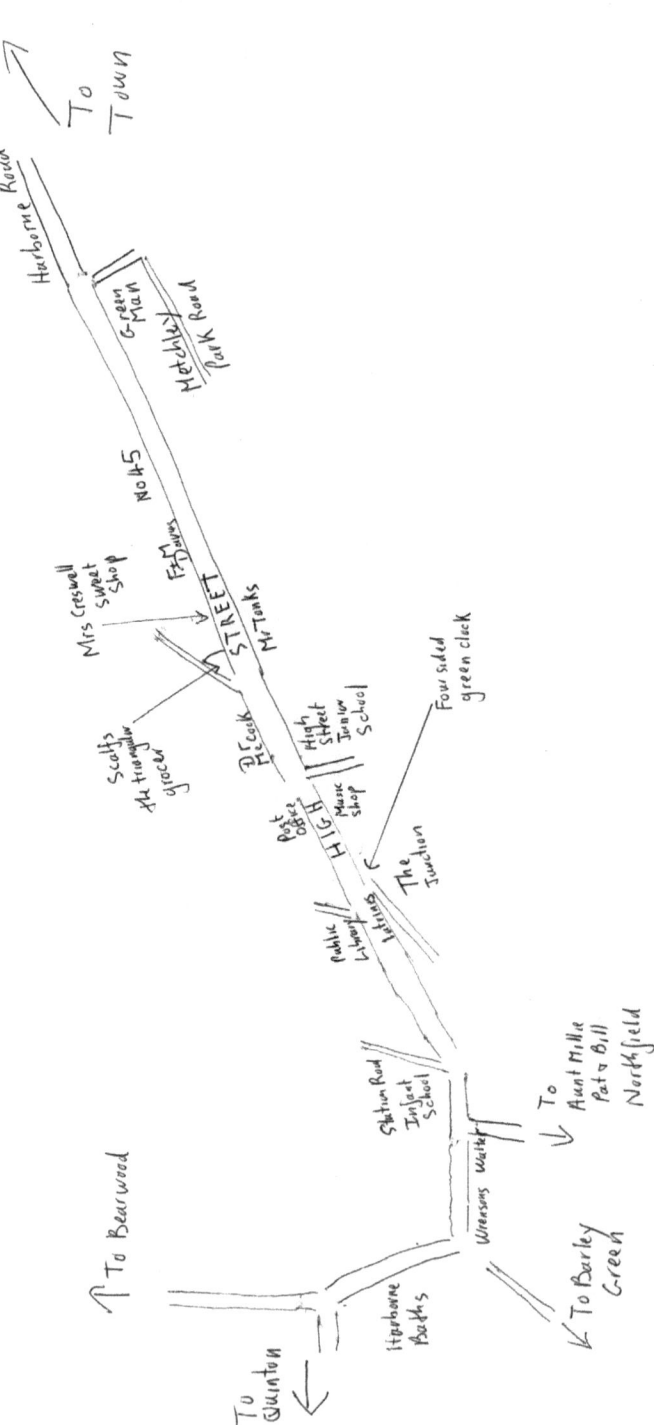

Quinton

Warley Woods

To Horborne

Blind School Road

Oak Court Road

the Queens Park

tall swings

roundabout

Midland icecream shop

Prefabs

To Bartley Green

Buston Road

Approved School

My house John's house

Norman Avenue

Co-op Grocers + butchers

Wolverhampton Road

To Carlisle

Grass

the Boulevard

Wolverhampton Road

The hunting grounds of the plains Indians

Grass

Mary Lucy Millar (1911–2001)
Charles William Millar (1914–1974)

For

Tom
Lucy
Sam
Hugo
Jemima
Leo
Alfie
Saba

ACKNOWLEDGEMENTS

This work was conceived in 2014 following my 71st birthday. Ideas are not little innocents. Sometimes an idea arrives that has been hanging around for a long time, asking to be teased out anew. Sometimes an idea arrives with no warning to put the knife in. And scrubbed ideas leave their trace. Leaving much more than a trace are ideas from present and past members of the British Society of Psychoanalysis, some acknowledged and many not.

Two works were essential to my writing.

A letter to John Steiner from Ignês Sodré, quoted at the Melanie Klein Trust Conference 14th June, 2014, in which Ignês Sodré describes the Fall from a psychoanalytic point of view. In: *Illusion, Disillusion, and Irony in Psychoanalysis* by John Steiner (Routledge 2020).

A paper by Ronald Britton, 'The preacher, the poet and the psychoanalyst'. In: *Between Mind and Brain: Models of the Mind and Models in the Mind* by Ronald Britton (Karnac 2015).

The ideas and comments of many people have contributed to this book. I want to thank Andrew Millar my brother, Bronwen Maxwell my sister, Lizzie Harding my daughter and my sons Ben Millar, Josh Millar, to whom I am very grateful for the book's cover design and photographs, and Jack Millar. I am also grateful for the encouragement at different stages of Ed Cripwell, Alex Harding, Bruce Addis, Richard & Gill Rusbridger, Tara Naidoo, Marie-Ange Wagtmann, Nick Bury, Anthea Foster, and Michael & Aimee Birnbaum.

I am very grateful to three artists for permission to reproduce works integral in the making of the book: Chris Orr (www. Chrisorr-ra.com) for *Norr Saws* (2006) on the book cover; Anthony Whishaw (www.anthonywhishaw. com) for *Dungeon* (1997-1999), *Post* (1994-1995) and *Baz* (2006); and Alice Mara (www.alicemara.com) for *Old Peoples' Home* (2010) and *Curved Building* (2015)

I thank Faber & Faber and Macmillan for their permission to include Seamus Heaney's poem In Time *for Siofra*; and Gillian Clarke for permission to include her poem Swans; the Oskar Reinhart Collection 'Am Römerholz', Winterthur for permission to reprint *The Adoration of the Kings in the Snow,* 1563, by Pieter Bruegel the Elder; and Tamar Schwartz of IPBooks for her help in bringing the book to publication.

I want to express heartfelt thanks to Karl French, my editor, for his faith in me and this work.

I want to express my gratitude to Mike Brearley, Jon Stokes, Nick Temple, and David Tuckett, with whom I have enjoyed many conversations and learnt much.

I am profoundly grateful to Claire Cripwell, my wife, for her love and forbearance with my long preoccupation with this work, not without cost.

CONTENTS

INTRODUCTION

Opening my front door, I am horrified to find Jim, ten years old, having a fit, tangled up in the wires of the Wi-Fi router. It is a consequence of modern breeding practices that gives pugs an appearance that limits their ability to breathe, squashing flat the structure that makes up the nose. William Hogarth's beloved pug, named Trump, in *The Painter and His Pug* [1745] in the Tate— has a pointed face. I untangle him, body rigid, mouth wide-open and panting, legs collapsed, take him tight in my arms, and sit on a sofa. He is looking at my face, trembling, front paws pressing fiercely against my chest. *Jim, it is going to be all right, it is going to be all right, it is going to be all right.*

I think about Baz, his fits and his wiry hair, a bit of a ragamuffin. The idea was that a puppy would give Baz a new lease of life. *Jim, he felt she had given up on him, had taken herself away, and he fell ill. When the vet and Angela the nurse came, we were all together in the kitchen,*

Baz in her arms, you sitting on the floor, telling him how much we loved him.

I feel Jim's body calming down. He jumps down from my lap and walks a bit unsteadily to the table on which his biscuit tin sits. He cocks his head and looks at me.

It is not always thus. As my family like to remind me, when they returned from the breeder in Evesham to collect Baz, carrying the puppy up the steps into the house, I was putting the rubbish out, in no hurry to say, "Hello."

This work is a tale of David, a boy from Birmingham, born in the middle of the war, looking back, while trying to make sense of the present. It is written in the spirit of Sigmund Freud, a thinker who engages with what he writes about close-up, where you see certain ideas coming back, patterns, not a system—patterns of ideas (beliefs about the world and our situation) built up from childhood experience that are inaccessible and kept unknown from us, because we are resistant to their felt implications. The patterns may be inferred, an intuitive guess, but the interpretation is always provisional, may be delusional and always requires evaluation.

The tale has had a long gestation, with much waiting and listening, with little connecting points taking me to places that transcend where I began. It is a tale of two worlds that are *our world.*

We inhabit a limited and limiting world, with deep foundations in experience of goodness, where reality forces us to relinquish possession of its source; a world where we experience hard-to-bear feelings and internal conflicts, where ambivalence—our positive, loving feelings and negative, hateful feelings towards a person or situation—is managed; a world where hate and aggression are active but where feelings of sorrow, guilt and anxiety become part and parcel of love, and where we do all we can to make something better to the extent that it is possible in reality.

And we inhabit a world of a spurious higher power, an internal tyrant believed to deliver authoritative truth, which invades to occupy, which demands propitiation while holding out the promise of a permanent state of wellbeing, a dream; a world where the longing for love is replaced by a longing for power.

Through a tale of David, I weave the notion that in each of our unique human minds is a connecting door to goodness; a connecting door to creativity, embedded in the universe from its beginnings, expressed through different kinds of medium, where one thing may get into another thing to create something new. There is a quantum of hope.

And I weave the notion of a subjective experience of connection and its catastrophic loss, of being insig-nificant, that creates havoc. I think we all have a bit of it.

I mean *havoc* in its old English, medieval French sense, where *cry havoc* is a shout that went up to pillage the enemy during defeat in battle, a violent devaluation and dispossession.

A tale of David tells of his attacks on a connecting door through which his mother goes to work on the home front in the newspaper shop of her dead father; of his dread of a coming to light of his underlying, unconscious, catastrophic belief that he has injured a connecting door to goodness, that he has made his mother depressed; of his adolescent conversion and ordination to a higher world, a counter-belief system that he treats as knowledge. It is a tale of falling, of havoc, of grief, and a depressive coming down as after the excitement and destruction of war.

I think a tale of David, where I am looking back, drawing on memory, on incomplete information, feeling my way, trying to make sense of the present, imagining possible alternative futures, could reach beyond the narrow confines of me.

There is no such thing as "Never Again". We face together many existential problems. The era of reconstruction in the years after I was born following the war, and more recently the Good Friday Agreement, emerged in part out of feelings of sorrow, guilt, anxiety and reparative wishes, a coming down following the excitement of destructiveness. Today we see gathering havoc brought by manmade climate change, loss of ecosystems, and the coming of war again to Europe—bringing an avalanche of tears.

"The Tibetan plateau happens to be the largest water tank in the world. All the major rivers of Asia including the Ganges, Karnali, Brahmaputra, Indus, Sutlej, Irrawaddy, Salween, Yellow River, Yangtse and Mekong—originate there. More than 1.5 billion people live by these waters: one fifth of the world's population. Without water, there's no life. If Tibet's 46,000 glaciers continue to melt, we will face unimaginable water problems and water will probably become a key cause for conflict in the future." (1)

Once, I met the Dalai Lama on the road. Well, I say I *met* him. It was August 2007—the summer before my retirement from my NHS job at the Tavistock Clinic—on a small road in northern Ladakh. We heard he was coming and were keeping a look-out. He was in the back seat of a car driving very slowly. We waved. I have a photograph I took of him looking at us, smiling, waving back. On March 17, 1959, following the uprising by the Tibetan people against colonisation by the Han Chinese, the Dalai Lama leaves Lhasa, fleeing on foot over the Himalayan mountains. The Dalai Lama says "No" to occupation. He sticks to his last.

On 7th September, 2017, returning from summer holidays in Donegal, I visited HomePlace in Bellaghy, the home village of Seamus Heaney. I find myself coming back, drawn to *In Time*, a poem inscribed on the wall, written for his granddaughter Siofra.

A voice comes over my shoulder: *Would you like me to tell you a story about it?*

Very much, I say.

The owner of the voice tells me it is from a reliable source. The poet was out having lunch with two friends and his wife, Marie. *Seamus*, she reminds him, *you have written a poem for your other two grandchildren but not one for Siofra.*

I'll do it now, says Seamus, who goes off to find a quiet corner, and returns with a piece of paper with the poem some twenty-five minutes later. What the poet wrote twelve days before he died is what is written on the wall.

In Time
for Siofra

Energy, balance, outbreak;
Listening to Bach
I saw you years from now
(More years than I'll be allowed)
Your toddler wobbles gone,
A sure and grown woman.

Your bare foot on the floor
Keeps me in step; the power
I first felt come up through
Our cement floor long ago
Palps your sole and heel
And earths you here for real.

An oratorio
Would be just the thing for you:
Energy, balance, outbreak
At play for their own sake
But for now we foot it lightly
In time, and silently.   *18 August, 2013* (2)

IMAGINE

Friday evening, November 1939, blackout material covering the bathroom window, black and white squares and diamonds, a candle sitting on the stool, extravagantly deep, steaming water from the electric immersion tank, his sandy head on the low wicker chair's pink cushion against the taps, asleep—arms hanging over the side of the cast iron bath with its four feet, Mary's right hand laid on his left leg.

You poor boy, we will not talk about it again, your haunting by your home, that is too much, as it is too much for me to say the three words you long to hear, an absence that I know pierces you again like nails. You took me east but not east enough. I would have screamed and shouted but I wanted you to take me right away. You bring me back here, saying it is a lovely little house and war is coming. War is here now, waiting outside our little house to take you away. You say I can go home. You do not see my fury and fear, horrible feelings buried deep inside me drawing me to the terror and its cruel nails—a darkness where I believe you do not want me, that I have driven you away. I want your baby, good Charles, awake, awake.

MINDING THE SHOP

Once, High Street Harborne village descended from the Junction with its green cast iron latrines in the wall just below the bus stop, four-sided green clock, and public library, to the music shop from where, later, I will buy my record player, the large Post Office, and High Street Junior School, from where my mother walks the short distance home from school to the shop with horrible anxiety—*Please let them not be arguing, let it be all right at home*—her parents barely speaking to each other apart from necessity.

Mrs A. M. McGowan, Headmistress of High Street Junior School, claps her hands, stopping "All things bright and beautiful, All creatures great and small". "I hear a voice singing out of tune and I think it is you, David. Come to the front, and don't open your mouth."

Mr Shuttleworth—who takes the 11+ class—picks up his thin cane, takes the boy out of the classroom, shuts the door. "Hold out your hand…" Swish. "…the other one…"

Swish. Teacher and boy—with stinging hands, trying to hold back tears—return to a silent class.

Past Dr Dora McCook's surgery, her waiting room with its hard, wooden pull-down seats full of coughing people, her clear-as-a-bell Scottish cadences as my mother comes again with her worries that I am not eating: "How's wee David today?" "Wee David is fine," she announces to my mother. Past the veterinary surgery, blown to bits by a bomb, the High Street bottoms out with Mr Tonks, the garage with its black taxi, then climbing, all in a row, Mr and Mrs Scalf, the triangular corner grocer, Mrs Creswell's sweet shop, No 43 "F&M Davies" the Wool shop, then No 45 "A Davies", then still more steeply up to the *Green Man*.

Shedding its village high street beginnings, the Harborne Road makes a long, sharp descent past Mr Hudson, the dentist, getting too old for the job, past the site of what will be the new secondary modern school, which I know I must not go to, then climbing again through posh Edgbaston, with its Botanical Gardens entered into through the hot Lily House with its noisy parrots; on to Five Ways with its much taller, four-sided green clock, and King Edward's Grammar School, with the slums of Ladywood hidden in open view; then down Broad Street with the Kunzle restaurant where sometimes on a Wednesday afternoon (half-day closing) mother, Aunt Florrie and Elsie have cakes and tea and I have an ice

45 HIGH STREET with my grandfather Arthur in his shop coat

cream, and then the columned town hall, concert hall, big library, and New Street—its station noisy with steaming locomotives and its lost, bombed, glass roof. Sometimes, a walk across the station to a huge wholesale place, with networks of tubes in the sky carrying dockets and money in brass bullets propelled by compressed air and returning receipts, where Florrie orders more wool for the shop and each New Year buys me a Harris Tweed sports jacket. Then left into Corporation Street and, at the corner of Lewis', the department store, left into Bull Street, and at Snow Hill Station to the north, left yet again into Colmore Row with St Philip's Church, since 1905 the cathedral church of the new diocese of Birmingham, from where the bus makes its way back to the shop.

I live at No 45, born to hard-working, lower-middle-class parents, with my mum, grandmother, called Nan by everybody, and Aunt Florrie. I am a new citizen of Great Britain, a country at war. All of us depend on the leadership of Winston Churchill, Franklin Roosevelt, and the despot Joseph Stalin.

My grandfather Arthur died of heart disease aged 65 years on 22nd January, 1942, 13 months before I was born. He had angina and suffered a weak chest from a gas attack fighting the Germans in France in the Great War. His father, Hugh Davies, was a tailor and draper. In the 1871 census, his mother, Anne Jane, born in Liverpool, is 32.

Hugh and Anne Jane married in Conwy on 31st July, 1861. Arthur was born in 1877 at 19 High Street, Conwy, Caernarvonshire, the youngest of seven children. By the time of the 1881 census, before Arthur is four, his mother is dead.

My grandmother Lucy was born about 1875, a Shropshire girl from Shrewsbury who became an apprentice dressmaker in Conwy. A Singer sewing machine is in her bedroom at the shop.

My grandmother's parents, John and Harriet Smith.
They look like quite a piece of work.

Arthur and Lucy married in 1899 and lived in Oswestry, Shropshire, close to the Welsh border. There is a misogynistic story, in which Arthur—who himself loses his own mother before he is four—threatens to shoot himself if Lucy would not marry him.

A studio photograph of their four children born in Oswestry, smartly dressed, hangs over a rose bowl in the back room of the shop.

Bill, Millie, Florrie, Percy

Harborne Bowling Club
Rosebowl Handicap 1936
Winner
A Davies

My mum, Mary, is not in the picture. She was born in Wrexham on 13ᵗʰ October, 1911 and was just three weeks old when the family moved to the Birmingham suburb of Bearwood, where Arthur worked as an insurance agent. Birmingham was a growing town, granted city status by Queen Victoria, where between 1891 and 1911 the population increased from around 478,000 to 840,000.

A year later, the family moved to Harborne. The money to buy 45 High Street was left to Arthur by his Aunt Jane, about whom I don't know a thing. That was a great piece of luck but not so lucky was the Great War that a very few years later swept up Arthur with so many others.

What I think of in my mind as the back room of the shop is actually a big room, the living room. The wall with the photo of the children divides the living room from the shop. To the right of the photo is the connecting door that opens, down three steps, into the shop. In the middle of this wallpapered room with its large carpet are a sofa and armchairs in front of a large fireplace. On the left of the wall opposite the photo is a large window looking into the back yard, and the door to the kitchen and scullery.

Against the middle of the wall is a heavy gate-leg dining table and chairs.

I have carted the gate-leg table with me on many journeys. Twenty-five or so years ago, a French polisher did with it what he could, but it is the Edwardian ugly it has always been. I've tried to get rid of it. Nobody wants it, not even the junky antique shop up the road. The owner offered £20, before leaving a phone message to let me know that it was not worth collecting. I think about taking it to the section for unwanted objects in Islington Council's recycling centre but can't bring myself. It is the table I am writing on. At least it has a job again.

On the table, Jim asleep with one eye open on his red cushion underneath, is *The Economist* for 27th February, 1943, the day I was born. The Beveridge Plan is not yet in the bag but, even at war, our parliamentary democracy is alive and kicking. The lead article, *The Debate Continues*, reports that the previous week in a Commons Debate, 119 Members voiced their protest against the government's faint voice by a hostile vote; the question "Has the Government accepted the Beveridge Plan?" remained unanswered. The Beveridge Report, published in November 1942, tackles *Five Giants on the road to recovery,* identified in bold capital letters: WANT, DISEASE, IGNORANCE, SQUALOR, and IDLENESS. The spirit with which the report is imbued was due to Mrs Jessy Mair, whom William Beveridge married a few weeks later.

Come on, William. How I hope you are going to be able to preach against all bastard-ing bastard gangsters who for their mutual gain support one another in upholding all the rest. For that is really what is happening still in England. (1)

My dad, Charles, came from Carlisle, where Hilda and May, his older sisters, still lived. Their father, who worked on the railways, died of pneumonia when my dad was just three. Their mother died when he was sixteen. There was "not the money" to enable him to stay on at Carlisle Grammar School, and he "worked in retail". This is the sparse story I received of his early life.

Dad (on the left) with three chums in Carlisle

Dad was 21, five years after his mother died, when he comes to Birmingham, with lodgings in Harborne, and a job as an assistant at Thrussells, gents' tailor and outfitters in Bennets Hill, off New Street. On black-tie occasions, I like wearing his thin gold cufflinks, engraved CWM, which I imagine were a present for his 21st birthday on 18th March, 1935 from his sister Hilda.

My parents met on a walking holiday in Derbyshire and danced on New Year's Eve on a wooden floor laid over Harborne Baths. Reports have it that Dad and Arthur took a shine to one another. Mum and Dad married on 6th June, 1938 in St Peters Parish Church, in old Harborne village, by the Bowling Club. Mum's bridesmaid was her best school friend, Winnie, a kind, shy woman who married John, a gentle, extraordinarily mild man.

For a year or so my parents rented a house in Sheldon in east Birmingham before moving back nearer Harborne and took out a mortgage on a house on Norman Avenue, in the newish suburb of Quinton. My cousin Pat hates the Davies'. "They are tyrannical. They think they're better than other people. Your dad should have taken your mum right away from the Davies'." Why doesn't he have the fight?

Mum and Dad somewhere at the seaside 1939

Number 37 Norman Avenue is a small inter-war, semi-detached, three-bedroom house in a quiet, tree-lined street. It has a front garden, a paved drive, the entry, that goes up the side of the house to a wooden garage, and a back garden with grass, and borders in which my father plants dahlias, which in the winter he stores in the shed at the bottom of the garden with its tall, swaying poplar trees, and the bathroom tiled in black and white squares and diamonds.

Dad in uniform, Queens Park 1940

Hitler's war begins with the invasion of Poland on 1st September, 1939.

The first group of Polish airmen arrived from France on 6 December, carrying all their belongings in suitcases, greeted by Kingsley Wood, Air Minister.

At the height of the Battle of Britain, one in five of all pilots in the air defending Britain were Polish. Hugh Dowling, Commander-in Chief of RAF Fighter Command said, "Had it not been for the magnificent material contributed by Polish Squadrons and their unsurpassed gallantry, I hesitate to say that the outcome of the battle would have been the same." By destroying 126 enemy aircraft in 42 days, 303 Squadron became the most effective Allied unit in the Battle. The King went to RAF Northolt to congratulate the squadron's fighter pilots. *From an exhibition on the railings of the Embassy of the Republic of Poland, Portland Place, London, September 2020.*

My parents let the house to a couple who promise to move out when Father came back, but there is nothing in writing. My mother returns to live at the shop. In the attic of the shop is a cylinder, attached to a foot pump. The idea is that I am to be put inside if there is a gas attack. Some loving hands, fearing the worst and hoping for the best, have stuck on it a transfer of Mickey Mouse. It seems unlikely the authorities delivered the cylinder with the Mickey Mouse transfer.

My father enlists on 15th March, 1940 in the Royal Corps of Signals. He sees me twice, a week after I am born and six months later, before he leaves on a troop ship. It must be so hard for him, not to be able to be with his family and to see me.

SGT. C. W. MILLAR
2591990
76 Div. Signals
Home Forces
For 27 Feb. 44

Dear Sonny David,

Although you are only one, and cant read or understand what this is all about, as this is your birthday you must have a letter. You see in the little family you belong to we always send a letter to each other on birthdays, just to say how much we love them, for sometimes we don't always say all those nice things to each other that we ought to: so just in case we have forgotten anything we send this special letter.

Well your mummy and Daddy think you are quite a lad, and are very proud of you. We hope you equally approve of us, for you are entitled to your opinion as a little individual, leaving that however to future years to show; when we look at you now, and I think of the little bundle you were just a year ago, we almost regret you are growing so fast, for we must admit to you in strictest confidence, that you have been a very good baby, you have given us so much to talk about, and so many smiles and happy hours David that you repay us for all our trouble and care.

Oh yes young man you are quite a lot of bother, and we might suggest you make this years immediate aim "no need for nappies," however sonny all we ask of you as you grow up, is that you will be happy in your mummy and daddy, helping us to be happy, and adding your love to ours in making one happy family; never be afraid to show your love David, many a heart has broken for thoughts that were never expressed.

So sonny as you go on to year number two, go on growing bigger, learning your new tricks, (and for mummies sake don't learn too many trying ones) so that your daddy will be able to show you all sorts of exciting things to do when he comes back.

Look after your mummy and be good to her, till daddy come home, my special love David and kisses, and very many happy returns of this your first birthday.

Your loving
 xxxxxxDaddyxxx
xxxxxxxx

X One big one for your birthday.

From the left, back Florrie, Mac, Elsie
Front Millie, me, Mum, 1944
Back yard of 45 High Street

By the time I come along, Millie, Bill and Percy have long left home. Percy is married to Muriel who wears furs and a smart hat. The couple show up not so often, but when they do, others talk together knowingly, about what I do not know. I like Uncle Bill. He is kind, with a lovely smile, a deep voice and a sense of fun. He drives the buses and is married to Hilda (a different Auntie Hilda to my dad's sister). Millie, the eldest, is separated and lives in a council house in Northfield.

Everybody smokes. Dad and Millie smoke the most. Mum and Florrie smoke posh *du Maurier,* packed in slim, pink-red boxes. Mum says that she had no wish to smoke when pregnant, which is lucky for me. Dad smokes Players Navy Cut. At Christmas there are boxes

27

of fifties and hundreds in the house, presents from his customers.

Millie says one Boxing Day, the family gathered in her house, in one of those conversations among the grown-ups that children listen to and remember, that she loved having children as babies but not after that. It stays in my mind. An internal tyrant can be passed down the generations. Is there an internal tyrant in Millie's mind, attacking connection with her daughter Pat with a mind of her own? Is there a tyrant in Nan's mind, in Mum's mind, in my mind? We may be occupied by an internal tyrant without knowing it.

From left Elsie, me held by Winnie, Grandma—Pat and Florrie at the back—Millie, 1944

Mum and I go out for a walk every afternoon and Pat sometimes comes with us. Pat loves my mother. I love Pat. She is wild and loves Ella Fitzgerald.

Mum and me, Metchley Park Road, 1945

Pat says she envies and hates me for being very loved by everyone, but she loves me too. She works in the Post Office, not any old Post Office, not even the large Post Office in the High Street, but in the big Post Office in town where there are lots of people. Pat has a lot of friends. She finds for herself Bill, a confident person—in the air force as ground crew because of his colour blindness. He takes her right away from the Davies'. Pat and Bill have lots to say for themselves. Bill, a plumber by trade like his father, Mac, becomes very successful and is much liked and respected. He later enjoys joking, or not joking, that I will never have a "proper job".

Bill is the son of Elsie and Mac, who live at the wool shop next door, F&M Davies, number 43. Elsie is tall, intelligent, and perceptive with a distinctive, musical voice. She always has time for me. Elsie is best friends with Aunt Florrie and helps her to run the wool shop. Florrie loves Elsie—but this is not talked about—and is jealous of Mac who is fond of the *Green Man* at the top of the hill.

Bill on an airstrip (desert?), January 1945

Mum and Florrie tell me that, growing up, their mother told them she never did want to marry their father.

I remember Nan as bland. Later, going in the car with my parents to take her to stay with her cousin Lucy in Shrewsbury, I remember seeing a different person—talkative, lively, someone with a life of her own.

The owners of the wool shop, F&M Davies, next door to No. 45, are Florrie and Mum. Arthur, a Great War father whose wife wanted nothing to do with him, made a gift of this next-door property to his two youngest daughters still living at home.

The only time I see my mother sneer, it is at other women who, in her eyes, pretend they have something. At a school speech day in my teens, sitting with my parents, Mum says she hates having to rise and stand at my school speech day for the accompanying wives of the masters—"I don't mind standing for the masters but why should I have to stand for their wives?"

The reader may be thinking, *Oh, but isn't that just what Sigmund Freud thought, the "masculinity complex", where women are supposed to have the bizarre belief that men have got the goods, women are deprived of what matters?* The psychoanalyst Ronald Britton, describing this as Freud's greatest mistake, sees the masculinity complex as not a problem for women in general but a psychic position adopted by some women, where the self-definition is that of being father's daughter—a particular kind of relationship that some women have to their fathers that is at the expense of their relationship to their mothers.

Mum is a friendly person but, later in life, is upsettingly contemptuous of women who juggle to combine having a family with a profession or job, believing married women had a full-time job looking after home, children and husband. Looking back, in this aspect of her life, I think that Mum is occupied by an internal tyrant that looks down at her, sneering at her femininity.

On the gate-leg table are two copies of the *Pocket Atlas of the World* published in 1942. I pick one up, the one covered in brown paper and well-worn. The two atlases were a bright idea of my father. During the war, he has one copy, and my mother has the other. He is able to write, without falling foul of the censors, *I have got to page 30 of my book*. When Mum opens her atlas at page 30, she sees he is somewhere on the Indian sub-continent.

Father is demobbed in January 1946, when I am two years, 11 months. At "the return" I am just a few months younger than he was when he lost his dad. He comes home from Ceylon on a troop ship, one of the huge, fast ocean liners that, having to leave behind their inter-war promotion from migrant trade to first-class splendour, move allied forces across the world. He hates the interminable noise of the bingo-caller echoing round the ship: *11 legs eleven, 66 clickety-click*.

On the winter night of "the return", he arrives by train at New Street station, catching a bus to the *Green Man* to walk down the hill and into the shop. I remember the shop in darkness, packed with people, excited, waiting, me sitting on the big wooden shop counter holding a small Union Jack. One of the men posted as lookout, looking up the hill. A whisper: *He is coming.* There is dead quiet. In through the door he comes, uproar, lights on, shouts, cheers. He is in uniform, kisses and hugs my mum, and comes and picks me up from the counter. I don't remember a thing more, other than next day he takes me on the number 12 bus to Bartley Green where we have a long walk around the Reservoir. The following day, my parents leave to have few days together in London. I make a big scene.

Dad works a brief time in the shop, before he and my mum, sensing the family's jealous feelings about him taking over, decide he must find another job. He gets work as an office manager of a wholesale stationer firm run by Mr Lewis; not to be confused with Lewis' department store in town, or the John Lewis Partnership, which does not move into Birmingham until September 2015, part of the re-building of New Street station with a new glass roof, now permanently closed following the pandemic.

The wartime tenants refuse to move out and my parents go to the County Court. Under oath, the woman admits her husband's verbal promise to leave when my father returned from the war, and that is enough for the judge. The access to justice that is focused on what is fair and true, of great moment to my family, happens long before I am in a position to understand the importance of the rule of law, but I remember it.

The move from the shop to Norman Avenue happens in the summer of 1946. Mum is streamlined to go. She is full of the yearning for improvement that will later grip the fifties. She loves Formica, the hard and shiny wipe-clean wonder surface that conquers the world and wins her heart. Blue Formica is the surface of the new kitchen cupboards that Mr Bluit, who lives in Alma Passage opposite the shop, is making for the Norman Avenue house. My mother is small in height and I recall her stung and hurt, angrily complaining to my father that when she told Mr Bluit that the kitchen cupboards he was making were too high, he told her that they were standard height. Mr Bluit had indeed blown it, revealing a contempt of women and their place in the world.

Dad's army record shows him in the Royal Corps of Signals for the whole of the war. His discharge papers show him made up to Company Sgt Major in 1945, and classed as a cypher operator. 76. div. Signals Home Forces was a division of the Royal Signals. Looking at how the Royal Signals operated, and the work done by 76 div. infantry home forces training the home guard in Norfolk to make it look as if we might invade the north German coast, he may have been embedded with them to pick up on the effectiveness of the decoy. His Soldier's Service Pay Book (which does not give any details of pay, or where he was based, for obvious reasons) shows his promotion to Sgt before going to Ceylon in February 1944.

When I ask Dad one bedtime about being a CSM, thinking it was rather smart, he jokes that where he worked there wasn't anyone ranking less than a sergeant. Working with codes on the other side of a world at war felt pretty exciting to me. But the return is difficult. Dad loves me very much, but it must be hard enough returning to the woman who has given her love to their son for the past three years that he has been away, without having to reckon with this rival in the present.

At bedtime I ask him again and again for stories about the war, meaning of course about him. I love hearing him describe the procession of ceremonial elephants when he was in Kandy. One evening, he tells me a story about men in Ceylon, carrying their swollen genitals in a makeshift wheelbarrow thing. Only later do I understand he is describing a symptom of elephantiasis. I feel disturbed and persecuted by what is probably something of a warning from Dad not to get too big for my balls. I am unable to digest the violent rivalry that the Oedipal situation stirs in me. I cannot engage with my parents to have the fight I need to have, and perhaps find understanding. I have a learning problem. I shut down. I stop asking for stories about the war. But I stay curious about how Dad makes and fixes things with his tools on the bench in the veranda on the back of the house, looking over the garden. The thing he makes that I most admire is a strong, green and red, wooden sledge with brass runners on which we all go sledging in Warley Woods at Bearwood.

Before the move to Norman Avenue, my mother and Dr Dora decide my tonsils need to be removed. Looking back, it is unlikely it was necessary. Tonsillectomy was fashionable and a business opportunity. The operation is arranged to take place in a private nursing home in posh Edgbaston. Early in the morning, I leave the shop with my parents. My mind is focused on getting my parents to buy me a bus ticket, not required at my age, a wish they are happy to grant. This, of course, is my remembered past, not my unconscious past with God-knows-what fears of castrating attacks. The nursing home in Calthorpe Road is a huge old house set back from the road. It has a vast square room with a huge nurses' desk positioned in the middle and a lot of children in beds. A baby is standing in a cot, holding on to the side, crying. I am put to bed, and my parents say goodbye. They are upset and I cry as they go through the door, waving. I have no more recollections until the next day when I get ice cream, and my parents are allowed to visit. Visiting is highly restricted, and the authorities permit only one parent at a time to see their child. My father appears but I say I want my mummy. He is hurt. The story runs in the family for a long time. The third day I leave with my mother and father in Mr Tonks' black taxi, a rug over me. My only ride in it ever.

These were the days before the publication of the research and pioneering ideas on attachment, separation and loss by the psychoanalyst John Bowlby. John Bowlby was still working at the other end of the corridor in the adult department of the Tavistock Clinic when I started working there in 1982. His work came to prominence after the war through his publications, and became widely known through the moving, unsettling and upsetting films of children in hospital made by the psychoanalyst James Robertson and his wife, Joyce. It is only a few decades ago that hospital authorities, occupied by an internal tyrant, brushed aside the attachment between infants and young children and their parents. At this time, after the war, visiting children admitted to hospital was still harshly restricted, e.g., St Thomas' Hospital London: first month no visits, parents could see children asleep 7-8 pm.

My dad buys from Mr Lewis, his employer, an electric train set, no longer used by his own children. On Christmas Eve at our home in Norman Avenue, when I am fast asleep and Father Christmas has eaten the mince pie and sherry left by the chimney, Dad lays out the train on the floor of the front room, kept for Sundays, Christmas and suchlike. It is not a regular Hornby set; the scale is somewhat smaller, but it looks good, except that my father discovers that the engine does not work.

After Christmas, Dad tries to get the engine mended but is told it is irreparable. That was very disappointing obviously. But what I remember most is how the train set just hung around the house in its box, useless without a working engine, probably ending up in the loft.

My dad as a little boy with a large handmade wooden engine, his favourite toy, after his dad died

"Come on, David. That bastard-ing bastard Mr Lewis. We are going to town to buy a Hornby train set. Your mother doesn't like the 'never-never' but I will fix it."

Dad doesn't say that. He doesn't have the fight he needs to have. I wish I had said, *Come on, Dad! What is going on? You can "fix it".* But I am in a fix. I don't have the fight that I need to have.

Mum and I walk from Norman Avenue to the village most weekdays. We go down Balden Road, past the "Approved School" hidden behind the wooden fence and tall hedging. Sometimes I see the boys in their green uniforms going into or out of the school drive. That crocodile frightens me. Then down to the Queen's Park, one of any number of parks, squares and so on up and down the country named Queen's something or other as a memorial of Victoria's golden jubilee. But, in my mind, it is *the* Queen's Park.

Occasionally, at the shop on the corner of the park, Mum buys me an ice cream. It has to be from that shop which sells Midland ice cream, which is white, and not from the shop the other side of the road that sells Walls' ice cream, cream-coloured and disgusting. We sometimes go into the park with its enormously high iron swings with long metal chains attached to wooden seats which later I will pump up and up and up, flying higher and higher until almost at right angles to the ground, with such force you feel you will shoot off into the sky, and then higher still when the swing and its chains start to shake and wobble and it is time to come down to earth. For now, I love Mum pushing me on the high swings, and the wood-cladded, cast-iron, hexagonal roundabout—so heavy that later I will make it go amazingly fast—but now with Mum holding me, scooting it around with one foot.

Sometime in 1947, a row of prefabricated bungalows—*prefabs* as they were called—appears on the edge of one side of the park. About 150,000 were put up across the country between 1945 and 1948, to help with the housing shortage after the War.

People were initially suspicious of the temporary nature of the prefabs, and a great deal of effort went into promoting their benefits in exhibitions and on film. Prefabs were modern, spacious and well-designed with modern conveniences; a fitted kitchen, with refrigerator, cooker and water boiler, fitted cupboards in every room, indoor toilet and bathroom with heated towel rails, running hot water, a back boiler and ducted warm-air heating. ... these detached bungalows provided space to grow vegetables and flowers, and for children to play.

. . . .

[This was] a time when there was optimism that a better world could be created and that ordinary people who had fought for freedom and against oppression deserved a good quality home with every modern convenience.

Jane Hearn. Director of the Prefab Museum. In *the modernist* Issue 29, 2018 pp. 14-17.

It is so interesting now to learn about this thoughtful reparative national project, and the quality of materials used in the construction of prefabs. But I remember looking down on them. I believe my lower middle-class family is superior and the prefab-dwellers are inferior.

Then, off down leafy Court Oak Road, past Mr Cuffley the hairdresser where my father has his hair cut short and where I have mine cut less short, then past the Blind School with its large gardens. Here I am more curious. I remember seeing someone with a white stick walking nearby, thinking, *what is it like to be blind*?

We turn right, past Harborne Baths, to the top end of the village, Wrensons' the grocer. Wrensons' has wooden counters round the shop and lots of assistants who serve the customers. My mother has a small black hardback order book with her name on the front—Mrs Millar—in which every week she writes down the things she needs and gives it to an assistant in the shop. Each Friday, a Wrensons' van delivers a cardboard box. Unpacking it, she ticks off each item in her book. It is incredible in retrospect how she fed us from that little box. It is partly the rationing, partly the shortages that remained a big part of life in the forties, partly my parents' need to be careful—my father's salary is regular but modest—and partly my mother's hatred of credit. Credit is traditionally a privilege of the middle and upper classes, but the way she sees it, credit is the "never-never" (hire purchase) of the working class.

Then, down the village past the Odeon cinema, the National Savings Bank, Station Road Infant School, where I will go, to the Junction. There, we often call in to the library, up the stairs to the big, bright room where there are so many books. My mother returns one or two books to the librarian and finds another one and usually one for my father. They read a lot in the evenings, mainly historical and detective. Then, down past the Post Office to the wool shop. My mother, Elsie and Florrie have a cup of tea. I usually ask for tuppence to take to Mrs Creswell next door to get some sweets in one of her triangular white paper bags.

Then, back home on the No 3 bus from the *Green Man*, getting off at "the Boulevard", a big grass-covered roundabout, and walking north up the Wolverhampton Road. The thing about this part of the Wolverhampton Road is that there is no connection with Wolverhampton. Work on the road stopped when war came. It is a quiet dual carriageway with an enormously wide grass central reservation. It is part of the territory where John, my friend from two doors down, and I, safely play. Into the distance, south beyond the boulevard, the green reservation is the hunting ground of the plains Indians in our endless games of Cowboys and Indians. I have no clue about the violent dispossession by the Americans of the lands of the plains Indians.

IT IS UPSETTING TO SEE YOUR MOTHER CRY

Station Road Infant School has a warm, friendly atmosphere, except for the day we line up in the spacious, light hall for diphtheria vaccinations, everywhere reeking with the smell of the dish of purple methylated spirits that contains the needle used to jab our arm. I think this Birmingham education authority school must have had an enlightened headmistress. The classroom is bright and cheerful with drawings and pictures round the wall. The school has parents' evenings. My teacher in the second year, Mrs Gill, tells my parents that I appear determined to work out numbers in a way that seems peculiarly my own, but I somehow get there in the end.

Looking back, Mrs Gill is a good observer, alongside being positive and encouraging. We don't have to be Albert Einstein to find something vital in finding our own way, but she is putting her finger on a learning problem.

Ernest Schanzer, editor of the 1969 Penguin edition of *The Winter's Tale* (1) by William Shakespeare argues that

King Leontes' murderous rage flares in the first act at a particular moment when the queen, Hermione, gives him an honest, realistic picture of herself and her feelings as a woman. What happens in the play at that point is that after Hermione tells Leontes that Polixenes is willing to stay longer, Leontes says that only once before has she spoken to a better purpose. She asks him when that was, and then gives a reply that stirs violent feelings.

LEONTES
Why, that was when
Three crabbed months had soured themselves to death
Ere I could make thee open thy white hand
And clap thyself my love: then didst thou utter
'I am yours for ever'.

HERMIONE
'Tis Grace indeed.
Why, lo you now, I have spoke to th'purpose twice:
The one for ever earned a royal husband;
Th'other for some while a friend.

She gives her hand to Polixenes

LEONTES *(aside)*
Too hot, too hot!

44

On the evening of 28th April, 2014, I walk to Caledonian Road tube station, the people's station with its helpful staff and classical music for passengers waiting to be whisked along the Piccadilly Line. I am seeing the new production of *The Winter's Tale* as a ballet by the Royal Ballet at Covent Garden, choreographed by Christopher Wheeldon and scored by Joby Talbot.

Things begin with a summery Sicilian prologue as Leontes (Edward Watson), King of Sicilia, and his childhood friend Polixenes (Federico Bonelli), King of Bohemia, are reunited for nearly nine months. When Polixenes is due to leave the Sicilian court, Hermione (Lauren Cuthbertson), is visibly pregnant. Through Christopher Wheeldon's choreography, music, and dance, we, the audience, feel the palpable sexual attraction between the queen and Polixenes.

In this production, it is a moment where Leontes and Polixenes are standing on either side of Hermione, each with a hand on her prominent bump, that brings the shout, *cry havoc.* Watson's dancing becomes angular, his body painfully tightened and tense, the music increasingly jangling. Menacing shadows appear. We, the audience, feel horror and dread, fearful for Hermione, son Mamillius (Joe Parker), and the baby who is to come, threatened by an invasion where their voices have no right to exist.

In the first act of Shakespeare's play, Polixenes escapes back to Bohemia. Hermione gives birth to a girl. When the independent-minded Paulina brings the new infant to Leontes, he wants mother and baby cast into the fire. Paulina's husband, Antigonus makes an intervention. He makes an oath to carry and bear the infant

> To some remote and desert place…
> …and that there …leave it,
> ….Where chance may nurse or end it…

Mamillius dies. Hermione collapses and is taken off stage by Paulina who returns to tell Leontes that the queen is dead. Leontes falls into the hell of melancholia, devastated.

Hermione speaks in a dream to Antigonus about how things are and what he needs to do:

> Good Antigonus,
> Since fate, against thy better disposition,
> Hath made thy person for the thrower-out
> Of my poor babe, according to thy oath,
> Places remote enough are in Bohemia:
> There weep and leave it crying; and for the babe
> Is counted lost for ever, Perdita
> I prithee call't.

In the play's second act, sixteen years later, we are once again in a summery place, the kingdom of Bohemia, where reports of the "rare note" of Perdita, who had been found by an old shepherd and lovingly brought up with his family, reach the ears of Polixenes' son, Prince Florizel.

In Christopher Wheeldon's choreography, Perdita (Sarah Lamb) and Florizel (Steven McRae) fall in love, dancing among a new generation of sexy boys and girls, under a tree of life hung with gold and silver decorations. And then from this high comes a repeat of the earlier shift into murderous terror in Sicilia. Polixenes, who has learnt nothing from life, incensed at his son marrying below his royal station, pursues the couple, who flee to Sicilia.

The final scene is what most takes my attention in this production. Paulina's (Zenaida Yanowsky) statue of Hermione—"many years in the making"—is a statue of Hermione *together with* Mamillius. As Hermione comes down to earth, leaving behind Mamillius, her unmoving son, I see them both lost and gone for ever, dead as stone. I see the love of Paulina, her bearing, her remembrance, and her courageous husband, Antigonus, as a connecting door that is felt to rescue Perdita, invaded by a tyrant, counted lost forever; encouraging Perdita's desire to know what is going on, that is to say her curiosity.

Hermione: …Tell me mine own,

　　　　　Where hast thou been preserved?

　　　　　Where lived? How found…

Hermione's coming down to earth, is not a triumph but a *making things better* inasmuch as reality allows things to be made better—an epiphany, a "coming to light" of the exuberance of meaningful symbolic resurrection, *and* sadness that accompanies the incomprehensibility of death.

Like swallows, swifts pair for life. Living for an average of five and a half years, they return from Africa each spring to meet up at the same nest site. Pairs of swifts return to nest under the eaves of the house opposite my home near the beginning of May. One muggy June evening, the colony is high up, swooping around on the currents, feeding on insects. *Come here and see*, she says. I stand and look. I see nothing. Then down he or she dives, tearing through the sky at amazing speed, quickly under the eaves to the nest, to deliver an insect meal for hungry chicks. The top speed recorded for a swift is 69 mph; only a peregrine dives faster. A minute or so later, he or she appears again, diving down from the nest almost vertically before curving sharply to take off back into the feeding evening skies.

The number of small tropical migrating birds such as the nightingale, swallow and swift are declining, brought about by the disturbance and disruption of climate change. The evidence suggests that the problem is in their migration route and wintering place (2). When they try to refuel, the expected food is not there and they starve. In the case of the swifts, which refuel on the wing, the drop in numbers is very alarming. Their migration path goes via west Africa to their wintering place in south-east Africa, where, again, the effect of man-made climate change has reduced the insect population in the skies on which they depend. However, there is evidence that at least some swallows, adapting to climate change, are no longer taking the hazardous path of migration and are over-wintering here.

On 12th May, 2016, I am driving into town to the vet with Jim to pick up his smart new EU passport. The rules require Jim to be present to have his identification chip read at the time the passport is handed over. On the car radio I hear Jenni Murray, the presenter of *Woman's Hour* on Radio 4 talking with Gillian Clarke, National Poet of Wales, who is shortly to stand down from the job. Their conversation begins with Clarke reading the poem *Swans* from a new volume, *Selected Poems* (3). It is a poem about connection and its catastrophic loss. Murray says it had made her cry when she read it, and after the poet reads her poem on air she is, as she puts it, reduced to tears again. This is the poem.

Swans

She was brave in the bitter river,
the *Mary Rose*, doomed,
ice-chalice, lily in bloom.

Thaw, her feathers and bone dissolve in the flow
and she's gone, flower that floated
so light over death's undertow.

In lengthening light he patrols alone
Ferocious on his watery shore
where the nest from last year and the year before

has drowned to a dredge of sticks and sludge.
In full sail, his body ablaze, bridge
over unfenced water, he waits for her.

The voice on the phone said,
'He doesn't know she's dead,
There's nothing to be done.'

Now love rides the river
like a king's ship, all wake and quiver,
and I can't tell him, it's over.[1]

---

1 Gillian Clarke, Selected Poems 2016 Picador: London

Jenni Murray's tearfulness gives lots of room for Gillian Clarke to be able to respond to her question: "What was it you saw that made you write that poem?"

The poet describes how she lives in the country but also, periodically, in Cardiff in a 12th floor flat looking down the river Ely where, for eight years, she has been watching swans nesting on the river. There are some, she says, at exactly this moment, sitting on eggs on exactly the same place as they have done year after year, spring after spring. But there were two or three very cold snowy winters, and the river froze. All the birds left the frozen river. When they came back, only one swan returned. It was soon clear that he had lost his mate, the hen. So, she rang the swan rescue people who said, "He has not seen the body." I said, "You must bring him another swan." They said he wouldn't accept a nice new mate. He would drive her away. So, for a very long time he kept the river alone. It seemed to her a very sad story. But it also seemed wonderful that with birds like swans and swallows, as long as their mate is alive, they are together. The swan, if his mate is killed and he knows she is dead, he sees the body, he will then raise the fledglings on his own. Indeed, both the male and the female will, if necessary, bring up the babies all on their own. She was watching this creature after she realised she couldn't bring another swan to make him happy. She thought and thought about the dead body of the female swan, where up-stream somewhere, up in the hills, away from the ice, she must have sailed away from the frozen river, so somewhere far up-river were the beautiful bones, the beautiful body of the creature.

The unhappy swan cannot mourn because he has not seen the body of his hen. Through the medium of the poem, Gillian Clarke grieves the loss that the swan cannot grieve—"There's nothing to be done"—*and* creates the love that rides the river that raises the new.

From connection and its catastrophic loss, good lord, deliver us.

My mum and dad thought I would get over the return. But *Wee David is not fine*. He cannot mourn the relinquishment insisted on by reality of absolute possession of the mother as a source of goodness; he cannot manage his ambivalent feelings. I think that the return begins not with my father's return but with my mother's father's return. Early morning, Mother goes through the connecting door to the shop, A. DAVIES, to work on the home front, leaving me in the back room with my toys, a bland grandmother, who I could have made more of, and the heavy gate-leg table. Heavy piles of newspapers delivered in the dark of the morning, tied with sisal, wait on the wooden floor for her to sort, put into smaller piles on the wooden counter, each paper needing to be marked with a road and house number— waiting for the paperboys to arrive, sometimes dashing late, picking up their pile, putting it into a canvas shoulder bag, and cycling off on their round before school.

My subjective experience of Mum going through the connecting door is not of a good mother who I love and I hate for leaving me, but of an internal, tyrannical mother who has given up on me, who has taken herself away. Like Leontes, I shout, *cry havoc*. I go into a sulk, attacking a connecting door through which my mother goes to work to keep me alive.

From connection and its catastrophic loss, good lord, deliver us.

Years later, when Mum was staying with me in London, I was laughing helplessly about something. Her eyes tearful, she told me it was a long time since she had heard me laughing like that. She always felt that my feelings for her changed from the time she had left me to do the newspapers; she felt I never forgave her. I am a tyrant.

"David, for Christ's sake, you don't have to sulk. I am not happy about it either but there is a war on. What about us taking some of your cars and bricks through to the shop and for you to play there?"

Mum doesn't say that. I wish I had made myself a big nuisance, instead of sulking. Mum might have taken my toys and me with her to play on a rug on the floor. But as Hemingway put it, "Isn't it pretty to think so?"

I inhabit a world of attachment and its catastrophic loss, occupied by an internal tyrant. I will no longer drink milk, only wartime orange concentrate. I love ice-cream and, later on, cream and cheeses of all sorts, but the smell of milk is disgusting.

In 1947 Christian Dior brings the New Look, and our home in Norman Avenue brings Mother's own new look. It is December and she is sick in bed upstairs. I hear her crying, telling Dad that she has been bad to him and that she is sorry. I remember feeling disturbed and frightened. I go into their bedroom to ask them if I can go and see if John can play—my friend from two doors away. Outside, it is shockingly cold, with dirty piles of snow pushed to the edge, as I walk the few yards to John's house.

We spend that Christmas with Florrie and Nan at the shop, with Mum ill in bed upstairs. Christmas is magical for children. And Christmas is a way of bringing people together that is very important to them. The family gather in the big room at the shop. A game we always played at Christmas, and I can't imagine it was any different that year, is the game of *ring on a string*, where it is always Mac's big ring that is called for. Everyone can play the game of *ring on a string*, from youngest to oldest. It cannot be purchased. The players sit in a ring—the spotter observing in the middle—watchful, receptive, intuitive, hands over the string, moving in synchrony with other players, hands coming together, touching, moving apart, touching hands on either side, coming together, and so on, in the work of ensuring the handing on of the ring (which can travel in either direction) until either a fumble (bringing hoots of laughter if the spotter is looking in another direction) or the spotter's informed intuition identifies a player holding the ring—signalling a changing of places between spotter and player, and so on.

Early January, Mum is admitted to Selly Oak Hospital. I am living at the shop when I start at Station Road Infant School. That first school morning, I walk from the shop up the High Street with Florrie and Pat, telling them about my persecutory anxiety (not of course that I knew such words), that I will be made to drink milk. Arriving at the school gates, the first things I see are crates of small bottles of milk piled up against the playground iron railings. Florrie and Pat sort things out with the teacher. I don't have to drink milk. I settle down—at school, I mean.

Mr Chambers, the consultant who delivered me by caesarean section, removes an ovarian cyst and tells her she is lucky not to have lost the baby.

Seeing my mother crying, telling Dad she had been bad to him, her illness that Christmas, her operation, and her pregnancy—these things happened. But the shocking cold and the piles of dirty snow pushed to the edge outside the house in my memory of December 1947 did not exist in external reality. My memory of the December of Mum's illness is elided with my memory of the terrifically hard winter and snow of January and February earlier in 1947.

My interpretation is that the shocking cold and dirty snow is part of a pattern of an underlying, persecutory, catastrophic belief that my attacks on a connecting door have injured her sexual connection with my father and caused her depressive moods. This hypothesis is a very big jump. Let me say more. One evening, back at Norman Avenue, Dad is very late coming back from work for supper. He is a reliable man. The hours go by—no message (we have a telephone). Mum becomes more and more agitated, pacing up and down. Her depressive moods are terrifying to me as a child. She can become a demon. I anxiously pretend to play with my toys on the floor of the dining room by the veranda door. I suddenly say—the words reverberate in my mind as I write—"Perhaps he is dead." Mum hits me around the head.

In this scene, it is likely that my father is actually having a fight of some kind with my mother. But I am enacting a model in my mind of a primal scene where I believe my attacks on the sexual link between my parents make me deserving of violent retribution. My two different sexual parents become a monolithic internal tyrant. I am in a fix, in a dungeon world where I cannot separate from my parents, where I cannot have a fight I need to have, and where I cannot bear feelings of sorrow and guilt.

Consider now a world, where toleration of hard-to-bear feelings of rage, humiliation, exclusion, envy, jealousy and the internal conflicts they bring—mourning the belief of absolute possession of the mother as a source of goodness—goes hand in hand with the beginnings of recognition of the loved other as a person with his or her own point of view. Melanie Klein writes:

> I hold the view that feelings of sorrow, guilt and anxiety are experienced by the infant when he comes to realise to a certain extent, that his loved object is the same as the one he hates and has attacked and is going on attacking in his uncontrollable sadism and greed, and that sorrow, guilt and anxiety are part and parcel of the complex relation to objects which we call love. It is from these conflicts that the drive to reparation springs, which is not only a powerful motive for sublimations, but also is inherent in feelings of love which it influences both in quality and quantity.
> Melanie Klein (4)

Ronald Britton (5) connects the transformation with

> the closure of the Oedipal triangle by the recognition of the link joining the parents [that] provides a limiting boundary for the internal world. It creates what I call a "triangular

space", i.e., a space bounded by the three persons of the Oedipal situation and all their potential relationships…

If the link between the parents perceived in love and hate can be tolerated in the child's mind, it provides him with a prototype for an object relationship of a third kind in which he is a witness and not a participant. A third position then comes into existence from which object relationships can be observed.

It is the coming into existence of a third position that enables the self to make judgements based on the authority of experience, and subject to modification. But this coming into existence is not a concrete possession. It is vulnerable to invasion by an internal tyrant. If we think we possess a third position then it has already become part of an idealised paranoid belief system.

In 1996, Dana Birksted-Breen (6) introduces the further idea that normally in the Oedipal situation, something that she calls an internal "penis-as-link"—in contrast to an omnipotent phallus, an internal tyrant—gets inside the mind; a structuring and linking function, configured in the mind of the child as a tripartite world of mother— linked with but different from the father—and child, that promotes mental space and thinking.

It is "penis-as-link", a structuring and linking function that gets inside the mind of the developing boy or girl, which allows a full symbolic capacity where we can treat a symbol, which is not the thing it symbolises, as if it is the symbolised thing, carrying its emotional charge. We can relate to a thing, internal or external, but also be separate from it. We can manage our ambivalence. We can empathise with a person who holds a point of view, different to our own, that we disagree with.

From connection and its catastrophic loss, good lord, deliver us.

Here is a story of a person who says "No" to an internal tyrant that invades. It is a story from the Mezzo-Soprano Janet Baker, Britain's greatest classical singer of the 20th century, told in her own words, of a complex interaction between her, Peter, her brother, and her parents.

In a 2015 BBC interview, Janet Baker (7) tells Antonio Pappano that if, in her opinion, she has done enough work, if the piece has been rehearsed well, and the production is going well, and she is happy with everybody and everything:

> there is this moment when you do stand aside, and something, I would use the word spiritual, puts the final touch on things, and then if the fates are with you, the magic can descend, which has absolutely nothing at all to do with you, you make the possibility, and that is what singing is, making the

possibility for something magic to happen, over which we have no control.

In a subsequent film (8) by John Bridcut, *Janet Baker in Her Own Words*[2], she describes how her brother Peter, four years older, was a very sick boy but he had a marvellous voice. When he was 11 years old, she accompanied him to an audition at York Minster:

> They came out of the room and said, "We would take you like a shot but your voice is going to break any minute now," and therefore it was too late. If he had gone at nine, he would have been in there. I felt the devastation of that disappointment very keenly for him.
>
> I knew my brother was sick all his life, sometimes in a wheelchair, with heart trouble. I didn't know he was going to die and my parents didn't tell me until the day he died which was the most devastating shock I have ever had in my life. And nobody talked to me. My parents didn't talk to me about it, nobody talked.
>
> I think I have been trying to make sense of that event ever since, never quite managing it. It was like laying an axe to our family life, laying an axe to a tree, cutting down something from which we never recovered. We all lived with it, but we were different people because of it.

---

2 BBC 4 14th April, 2019

The last day was very curious. This I regret my parents doing. They told me at breakfast the doctor said he was going to die that day. And I remember saying to my mother and father, "But I don't want him to die. I don't want him to die." And I thought in that moment they told me—we used to share my teddy bear when he was really ill—*Can I borrow teddy?* I envisioned immediately going up the stairs to him with teddy and talking with him and coming down again. I know that I had the courage to do that without upsetting him. I don't know how I knew I could do that. I knew myself better than my parents did because they sent me away for the day, down the road to play with my friend.

I was shut away all that day from something I knew was happening 50 yards up the road which was the most incredibly important thing that had ever happened to me.

At 6pm my father came and fetched me back. My grandparents had come over, and we all stood around him in his bedroom. He died very peacefully in my mother's arms. But the moment of that, having to watch it, and the moment afterwards, I don't know how on earth I ever sustained it.

Of course, immediately my mother took me in her arms and said, "Now you are all I've got," which I felt very keenly until the day she died. It is like a psychological burden had been transferred to me which I felt at 10 weighed very heavily on me. I took that burden at 10 years old and I carried it for the rest of my life.

This is a very personal memory, but it is interesting because it is such a formative one, that I feel has affected my life certainly as a performer, and I think perhaps as a human being as well. It was food in a terrible way for the kind of sensitivity I feel in my working life, a tremendous gift to me from him.

My mother used to say, "Peter left you his voice," and I absolutely refused to contemplate that. I said, "No. He had his beautiful voice and I had mine. My voice is nothing to do with anybody else."

When I was grown to 12 and 13, she would say that to me, "You've got Peter's voice." "I haven't got Peter's voice. I've got my voice." And I was absolutely secure in that knowledge. I wasn't a copy of anybody else. That was my gift. It had been given to me as his had been given to him.

Janet Baker leans forward, just slightly, looking at—and speaking directly to—the viewer:

It was the experience I suppose of deep, deep feeling, that he gave me the capacity to feel something that deeply.

Through her medium of singing, helped by the work and love of others, Janet Baker achieved the means that offered real choice—bringing changes to the boundaries of her self and what she was capable of. She creates symbolically new ways to go upstairs and share her teddy bear with her dearly loved brother Peter, talk with him, know what was going on, and come downstairs. Her achievement, "making the possibility for something magic to happen, over which we have no control"—a new thing—is work she shares with us, the audience. As she makes plain so movingly, this reparative work is at a cost. An internal tyrant cannot be purged. Its consequences may be modified but it never goes away.

DUNGEON
1997-1999
Anthony Whishaw

A HIGGLEDY-PIGGLEDY FALL

I pick up from the gate-leg table a copy of *The Wind in the Willows* by Kenneth Grahame—an attractive edition with maps published in 1954 by the Reprint Society. At the bottom right-hand corner of the front cover, Toad is grandly expounding about the world to his friends Mole and Badger.

Inside the book, Mum has written in the same royal blue ink always used by my father.

To David from Mummy & Daddy

Xmas 1954

To remind him of his part in the school play.

No *love*, I notice. It is not only with me she is stingy. Also lying on the table is *Captain Hornblower RN* by C.S. Forester (comprising *The Happy Return*, *A Ship of the Line*, and *Flying Colours*). Inside she writes, *To Charles with best wishes Xmas 1951 Mary*. Dad complains she can't bring herself to say, *I love you*, despite him trying all sorts of stratagems. Jim pushes the door open and curls up on the red cushion under the table.

Eleven-and-a-half, I go to King Edward's Five Ways School, Birmingham. At Friday assembly, the headmaster reads a collect—perhaps each Friday, or perhaps only on Founder's Day—for our "pious founder and benefactor", the protestant King Edward VI. We might have been more interested to hear that our Founder was a healthy 14-year-old until suffering a severe attack of measles and dying of complications the following year (1). Interested, but back then not scared because the majority of us, including me, had already had measles. (Vaccination for measles is not introduced until 1968.) Measles was commonly regarded as a benign disease of childhood. It was not known then that measles can attack the immune system. And during the '50s and '60s the number of deaths from infectious diseases continued to decline.

The school has a caste system. Following the 11+ examination, each of us enters as a little A, a little B, a little C, or a little D. I enter as a little B. There is a bit of a shake-up at the end of the first year, but little movement thereafter. I begin quite well but then I start slipping down the class and can't get my timing together to answer all the questions in the end-of-year exams.

But that first year shows one sign of confidence. At Christmas, the school puts on a production of *Toad of Toad Hall*. I want to be in it and love the gathering pace of rehearsals interrupting lessons, masters becoming masters of lighting, production, direction and stage management, and to me the strange, captivating sound of the school orchestra rehearsing away. On the three December nights of the show, the staff common room is taken over with trestle tables loaded with makeup and costumes made by our parents, organised by the Parent Teachers Association, presided over by the indomitable Mrs. Plant, whose home has central heating. We ferrets have white costumes with tails that we swirl and swish around fiercely to the Wild Wooders' songs.

Toad is a boastful creature, very pleased with himself. Empathy for the feelings of others is not his strong point, with his furious driving, smashes and rows with police. He goes too far, stealing a motor car.

"... all sense of right and wrong, all fear of obvious consequences, seemed temporarily suspended. He increased his pace, and as the car devoured the street and leapt forth on the high road through the country, he was only conscious that he was Toad once more, Toad at his best and the highest..."
Kenneth Grahame, *The Wind in the Willows*

Toad is sentenced by a tyrannical court to years in a dungeon. Meanwhile, as one of the archaic Wild Wooders, I have a high time making havoc—in accelerating fury, trashing and taking over Toad's home. But Toad, like me, is a lucky animal. He is helped by a kind, perceptive girl, who brings him meals in his dungeon, who Toad looks down on as an inferior, and by her aunt, a washerwoman. They give him the chance to escape and reach his good friends, Ratty, the water vole, Mole and Badger.

Ratty tells Toad that this time he had feared that Toad really was done for.

"... the Wild Wood animals said hard things, and served you right, and it was time this sort of thing was stopped. And they got very cocky and went about saying you were done for this time! You would never come back again, never, never!"

The end of my first school year, 12 years old, I attend a "Pioneer" boys summer camp by the sea in Anglesey—an evangelical Christian camp promoted at school by Jeremy, the handsome, rugby-playing Head Boy whom I had a crush on. I enjoy the camp and return several times. The third summer, Jeremy brings with him his attractive girlfriend, who helps in the kitchens. I have an evangelical conversion.

I think proselytization of adolescent boys, whether through this kind of evangelical camp or coercive hell-fire sermons at Irish Jesuit retreats, holds out a promise of permanent protection from the hard-to-bear feelings, which are stirred by the tumult of adolescent sexuality.

In the dusk of a beautiful summer evening, in the big tent lit with paraffin lamps hanging on ropes, with crusader songs, I know him when I see him, a young, ideal father.

Behold, I stand at the door and knock; if anyone hears my voice and opens the door, I will come in and sup with him and he with me (The Revelation to John 3.20).

It touches my underlying, unconscious, catastrophic belief. But I do not ask, *"Jesus hang on a moment, what the hell is going on? What is happening on that green hill far away where a violent tyrant is making use of Roman soldiers to drive nails into you and leave you hanging out to die?"*

Returning home, I try for a bit to hold little services of readings and prayers in the sitting room for my parents—projecting into them the vulnerability of my subjective experience of connection and its catastrophic loss, and my persecutory, catastrophic belief that I have destroyed a connecting door to goodness—but it isn't long before they get fed up with this little tyrant and rebel.

During the third school year, instead of falling as previously, I steadily gain ground, and do well in the end of year exams. But it needs chance to allow me the promotion. A 3A boy moved that summer with his family to Australia, leaving a place.

I move up to 4A, which had been prepared for some time to take three "O levels" in the fourth year, commonplace now but a new venture for the school at the time. I am near the bottom in the maths class. But Sam Hinton, the senior maths teacher, who I find quite frightening, is encouraging. My parents also help me by arranging private coaching one evening a week with Mr Maltby, a teacher who lives nearby. He has lost the lower part of his left arm. Is it a war injury? Was he born with it? I never think that I could ask him. I don't think he would have minded. But I do recall being curious and impressed by his skill at sharpening pencils. A kind, patient man, while he is able to do little to improve my dismal French, he helps my confidence with maths. It turns out a nice "O level" paper and I get a distinction, a big surprise. I am awarded a Foundation Scholarship. At 15 years, as at five years, I settle down. I become more confident, and for the first time feel part of a peer group.

Arrogance builds the road to the gate of the Buchenwald concentration camp. The gate reads on the inside, I learn from Neil MacGregor's *Germany, Memories of a Nation* (2) and the exhibition at the British Museum, "To each what they are due,"—a shocking juxtaposition. But looking back, I think my conversion provided me with a breathing space.

Cousin Lucy, who as a child I met just twice in Shrewsbury, with my grandmother, must have liked me. She leaves me a bequest of £360, a great deal of money in those days. The money enables me to buy a longed-for

Bush record player, helps me at university, and funds a wonderful journey in the summer of 1961 after leaving school. My parents are brave or mad enough to agree to me travelling pillion on the Lambretta of my school friend Bruce. Bruce has the gift of musicality and introduces me to classical music with concerts in the concert hall at the Town Hall. Motorised transport presents no obstacle to staying at youth hostels in Europe (unlike Britain at that time). The Germans shot down Bruce's father's bomber plane on a raid over Germany, Dortmund according to his Logbook, on 25th March, 1942. There were parachutes for the crew but not one for Bruce's father, a Sergeant Pilot in the RAF Volunteer Reserve. We visit the war cemetery at Kleve, the Reichswald Forest War Cemetery on the Dutch-German border, not far from Düsseldorf. Later, on 9th January, 1963, I go with Bruce and his lovely girlfriend and later wife, Ros, to the first secular performance of the *War Requiem* at the Royal Albert Hall, by the London Symphony Orchestra, Bach Choir, Highgate School Boys, conducted by Benjamin Britten and David Willcocks.

We travel down through Germany, Bavaria, Switzerland, and over the Brenner Pass. Coming down, passing any number of men trying to flog fake Rolex watches, I see for the first time the beauty of the plains of Italy below.

The Lambretta: taken with a Zeiss Ikon Nettar, Novar-Anastigmatic with Vario shutter, my pride and joy.

– then Venice, Rimini, and Florence, before the return along the coast to Cannes, then turning north through France.

Going up to King's College, Newcastle-upon-Tyne in 1961 to read chemistry, I am very happy there. I make good friends at my hall of residence—the grandly named Eustace Percy Hall, an absolute barn of a place with endless corridors, built during the war or before as a hostel for government workers—with a cheerful, lively group from Meth Soc.

My Methodist friends (I am the small figure top right)

In the University Rag week early that first term, I am atop the Meth Soc float in the Haymarket, filling paper bags from big barrels of flour and hurling them in the direction of anyone walking in the vicinity. I am delighted to finesse a flour bomb through the revolving doors of the Barclays Bank branch on the Haymarket. At 18, the readiness of the city to put up with such wildness feels like freedom to me.

Chemistry is my first experience of an apprenticeship. There is a lot of graft, but I love the immersion in the discipline's highways and byways. The weekday afternoons of a chemistry undergraduate are spent in the laboratory, a laborious, time-consuming world of experiments and write-ups to be handed in and marked by our teachers. We use the university library to revise in and the department library to consult as required but get a great deal of the stuff we need from lectures—usually in the form of revolving, chalk-filled blackboards—with which our teachers filled our mornings.

Study is divided for practical purposes into three domains—inorganic chemistry, organic (its molecules the building blocks of life), and "physical", an assortment of stuff like electrochemistry and crystallography. Little attention is given—or indeed is wanted by us—to the historical connections and prefiguring of our subject, although somewhere near the centre of my passion for chemistry is Mendeleev's periodic table—a hard-won mapping of what makes things tick.

In my second year, Dr McQuillan, Reader in Organic Chemistry, a somewhat austere-looking Oxford man not without a sense of humour, returns one of my hand-written write-ups, saying, "Ever write home, Millar?"

"Yes," I reply, tense, taken aback.

"Surprising," he says.

Let not the reader suppose that reading chemistry is rote learning. It is not possible to digest the vast amount of information, theories and sometimes hobbyhorses of our teachers (that we are wise to note), without beginning to build up many layered complex models of what might be going on in the molecular world. What are the chemical and electrical mechanisms? What is connected to what, what inserts what, what receives what, what combinations are strong, what are weak, what is the effect of the medium—hot, cold, acidic, alkaline, and so on?

In my final year, we are given a number of more complex experiments to carry out, a mixture of testing us and involving us in a rite of passage to demonstrate we can make something of it all. In the story I will tell, there is no need for the reader to understand anything about chemical reactions. Indeed, I cannot myself remember the details of the inorganic experiment I now relate. What may interest the reader—and why this all comes to my mind—are the circumstances. After three days' work, instead of arriving with the expected stuff, let us say a white compound, I end up with a yellow one. Going over my notes, I conjecture that at such and such a point I may have reversed the order of two procedures. I cannot be sure. What I can be sure about is that the yellow stuff is not the same as the expected white stuff and I have no idea of the chemical reactions that led to its production. I feel pretty dejected. It is far too long an experiment to repeat in this undergraduate setting but I roll my sleeves up and use the ideas, techniques and skills I have learnt over three years to analyse the chemical structure and properties of the yellow stuff and look at all the data available to me. I am helped by the fact that this data includes the known chemical formula for the white stuff that I had hoped to make.

The result of my investigation points to the very strong probability that the yellow stuff is an isomer of the white stuff. The concept of an isomer is long-established, describing a phenomenon where two compounds have the same chemical formula but the arrangement of atoms in the molecule of one compound has a different structure to the other, giving different properties. Mulling things over, playing with possibilities, I work out a likely molecular structure for the yellow stuff, which is consistent with its properties. I cheer up. Organic isomers are two-a-penny but an inorganic isomer not reported in the literature is more exciting, at least to an undergraduate in the 1960s. In goes the yellow stuff, with my write-up, to Dr McQuillan, and back comes an alpha+++, rather than the beta++ or occasional alpha I usually get for my lab work. It is a story of an imaginative new (for me) conceptualisation, even though it involves no new concept, and the yellow stuff, as far as I know, is of no practical use.

In 1964, in my last term, Leonard Wilson, the liberal Bishop of Birmingham, comes to talk to a Sunday evening congregation packed with students at the university church St Thomas' in the Haymarket. *Follow what you feel is true even if it goes against God or any other authority*, he says. I sense truth in his words. Leonard Wilson had been Bishop of Singapore when captured by the Japanese in 1941 and interned in Changi. For years, he led the Remembrance Day eve prayers at the Albert Hall, with poppies dropping in near-unbearable silence on the assembly.

At Newcastle, I have been accepted by CACTM, as it was then called, the national advisory body of the Church of England with oversight of the training for the ministry. I love chemistry but not enough to want to spend my life in a laboratory. I leave the molecular world of chemistry to go up to St Catharine's, Cambridge to read part 2 of Theology Tripos.

However, I don't know what I am doing. In the summer of 1963, before my final year at Newcastle, I do a placement at Dounreay atomic power station (now undergoing complex nuclear closure). There, on this northern tip of Scotland, I catch a glimpse of the existence of the Beatles, the four working class boys from Liverpool, whose music, talent, personality and teamwork created a new thing—youth.

A recent visit to *You say you want a REVOLUTION? Records and Rebels 1966-70* (3) at the Victoria & Albert Museum evokes strongly the music, art, fashion, and politics of those times. It is exciting, looking back at this period, to see the power of imagination to shake loose so many things, for young people to discover more of their own liberty, and a new sexual freedom. But in the '60s, I am out of it.

At Cambridge, with its wealth of all kinds, I find, of course, I am nothing special. My learning problem recurs. I am fascinated with and hungry for history and I choose all the history options—early church, the reformation, and 19th C church. But I am in danger of drowning in facts. It is back to the bloody B stream.

I fare better with the approach to the New Testament Gospels by Dennis Nineham, Regius Professor of Divinity.

Denis Nineham, following in the steps of German critics like Rudolf Bultmann, gives me a model—a portal that enables me to imagine, to see beyond the ostensible biographical and historical presentation. There is good evidence that the four Gospels—St Mark the earliest—were all written after around 67AD, when the Jewish revolt against the Empire led to invasion by Roman armies, destruction of Jerusalem and exile.

Denis Nineham writes in his commentary on *St Mark* (1963 Penguin), "What the Gospels give us, inextricably fused together in a single picture, is the historic Jesus and the Church's reactions to, and understanding of, him as they developed over half a century and more." (p. 51) They are made up of preaching material "intended to convey a religious message and demand a religious decision" (p. 52).

That is to say, what we hear of Jesus' life and teaching is the message the editors/gospel writers of the early church want us to hear in the context of their beliefs.

Dennis Nineham died in May 2016. So, I am taken aback when a few months later, in September, he returns to write an obituary in the *Guardian* of David Jenkins, onetime Bishop of Durham, a slightly younger contemporary.

Neither of the two men believes in the concrete resurrection. In other respects, the two are strikingly different as persons. Nineham is an intellectual and clear thinker, while Jenkins has a very roundabout way of thinking. Nineham says fairly, if a trifle unkindly, that Jenkins "made no claim to be a profound or original thinker, and words tumbled from him so fast that his colleagues sometimes found it hard to be sure what he was saying, let alone assess it fairly." But it appears from what Nineham says in the obituary that his return from the dead is prompted by him wanting to say something important about Jenkin's 1966 Oxford University *Bampton Lectures*.

"Entitled *The Glory of Man*, they were extremely well received. The focus was on modern interests and anxieties, and particularly on contemporary concern with what he called 'personalness'. He argued that man's personal liveliness points to his—derived and as yet largely potential—divineness. Anthropology, he suggested, implies and involves theology." (Dennis Nineham, *Guardian*, September, 2016).

Nineham twice complains that Jenkins never followed up his Bampton lectures. He is asking, *Why did you not follow up your own ideas?*

I remembered hearing David Jenkins, a year or so after his Bampton lectures, introduced by Robert Runcie, "the Boss", standing at the front of Graham lecture room at Cuddesdon theological college, which I attended for two years after Cambridge. And I recalled Jenkins standing there and his big roundabout way of thinking—but little more, I must say. I make some inquiries and discover to my surprise that Jenkins actually gave us several lectures! I am reliably informed he would drive to the common room door and park his Morris Traveller, staying with his pipe in the car for quite some time in clouds of smoke, before coming through the common room to give us his thoughts.

Ten minutes' search of my unsystematic bookshelves turns up my copy of the Bampton lectures, *The Glory of Man*, purchased from Blackwell's, undisturbed for the last 50 years. I find something interesting in the opening chapter:

> *If a man refuses to be concerned with persons in a manner which refuses to respond properly to the fact that they are persons, then he is refusing to face up to reality. P. 3.*

But to claim that a concern for persons as persons is, and must be, the central and universal ground for our approach to life is to fail to recognize the way in which so much in human affairs distorts and frustrates the development of persons. In particular, it is to ignore that there are good grounds for holding that each and every human being has built in as part of his or her personality elements which work against the production of a rounded and fulfilled personalness—either in the individual as a person or in those other persons with whom the individual has to do. (Lecture 1, p 4)

Denis Nineham's complaint—why did you not follow up your own ideas?—is made to the living. Hilary Mantel, an Honorary Distinguished Fellow of the British Psychoanalytical Society, in the course of a discussion following a talk *Lawyers, Mediums, Monsters* to the Society in June 2016, said:

We are always knocking into the dead and they are knocking into us. They are dead. We live not by becoming these other people but by getting in between, some place where we can ask questions and they can question us, *What are you doing?*

Jenkins was exploring in the '60s whether ideas from modern, foreign disciplines like anthropology and psychoanalysis might get inside the stories of an old discipline, theology, to create something new. For twenty years after leaving the church, I had no appetite to follow up Nineham's complaint.

Then, in the mid-'90s, the psychoanalyst Elizabeth Spillius, one-time social anthropologist, suggested I might be interested in the work of the social anthropologist Edmund Leach. This changed everything. Leach shows good grounds for holding that an underlying, unconscious belief of connection and its catastrophic loss, of an attack shutting a connecting door, covered up by idealised dogmas, is built into the Judeo-Christian tradition—a world of an internal tyrant opposing and working against the creative elements of the tradition.

During my last year at school, Dad left Spicers, "the paper people", for whom he had worked as a commercial traveller for many years, to buy a newsagents shop—following in the footsteps of Arthur Davies. Dad wanted his own business. It was hard work and went well. One of his contacts was the entrepreneur Ken Webb, who in the early-'60s, had grown Save the Children Christmas Cards, the first successful charity card business. It became a public company and made Webb a millionaire. Webb and a couple of others that we now call venture capitalists, who were looking to set up new businesses to invest in, offered Dad the opportunity to sell the shop to take a stake and manage a new mail order company for accountancy firms, called—of all things—Evrite. As well as being a business opportunity for Dad, Evrite was, I think, a dream.

The problem with Evrite is not that it carries too much risk, but too little. It is a steady earner, like my dad. Webb lost interest in the company. Well, business is business, but for Dad a dream is punctured. Side-lined by an unpleasant new management structure, he has a heart attack in the office, aged 51. He gets out, the only sensible decision, and re-joins Spicers' as Birmingham office manager. Dad is well liked there but he is very shaken.

Dad and I are falling.

I am following my dream. At a signal from the Precentor, at 11 o'clock, Trinity Sunday in the summer of 1968, the procession begins its migration from the great Chapter House of Worcester Cathedral, through the cloisters, with the haunting petitions and repetitions of Cranmer's Litany from the Prayer Books of King Edward VI

From connection and its catastrophic loss, good lord, deliver us.

snaking through the south door of Worcester Cathedral, the Verger, the Precentor and the choir of men and boys, those of us to be ordained deacon, including myself, and priest, many clergy of varying ranks, and bringing up the rear Mervyn by Divine Permission Lord Bishop of Worcester with snake head-dress. He lives in Hartlebury Castle and before lunch serves up the blackest of sherry that puts everyone at ease.

In James Joyce's *Portrait of the Artist as a Young Man*, Stephen gets the tap on the shoulder from the Jesuit director:

> – I sent for you today, Stephen, because I wish to speak to you on a very important subject.
> – Yes, sir.
> – Have you ever felt that you had a vocation?[3]

> He [Stephen] listened in reverent silence now to the priest's appeal and through the words he heard even more distinctly a voice bidding him approach, offering him a secret knowledge and secret power.[4]

An internal tyrant promises Stephen a high place of secret knowledge and power, if only he would devalue and pillage the connection between his sexual parents, a different order of relationship to the one he has with either his mother or father. That evening, Stephen returns home to his siblings. Neither parent is present, the table is poor, and Stephen's

---

3   James Joyce, *Portrait of the Artist as a Young Man* p. 157.
4   James Joyce, *Portrait of the Artist as a Young Man* p. 159.

siblings tell him that next day they will yet again be dispossessed of their home. Stephen has good reason for complaint. Yet, in a moving scene, the children around the table begin singing together, and Stephen joins in.

Unlike me, Stephen, in this scene from Joyce's novel, says "No" to his mind being colonised by an internal tyrant promising a secret knowledge and secret power and demanding propitiation. But I do not take a reductionist view of the awe I felt in that great procession on Trinity Sunday 1968.

On a pleasure boat, twin towers in the background, in Manhattan August 2001

Thirty-three years later, the remembrance of feelings of awe returns on a pleasure boat. It is a hot afternoon in August 2001—my first visit to New York. As the boat passes under the Statue of Liberty, I imagine myself a migrant on one of the ocean liners of the transatlantic shipping lines, who before the outbreak of war in 1914 were in fierce competition for the profitable migrant trade, approaching Ellis Island, gateway to the United States of America, and gazing up to the great statue reaching from sea to sky. Many migrants will have come from homes and groups escaping persecution, others from the grind of lack of work and opportunity. Others came from the grim starvation of the potato famine in Ireland, compounded by restricted thinking and a failure of politics in Britain.

True, the Statue of Liberty is not everything I imagine that summer's afternoon in 2001. It seems its making by the French is a lot about republican solidarity and little about the predicament of migrants. And at the statue's feet the sculptor Frederic Auguste Bartholdi has had to hide—and, even then, only after much argy-bargy—the broken chains and shackles of Afro-Caribbean people.

And three weeks after that day, the twin towers, so enormously tall and prominent on the skyline, fall with the destruction of so many lives. It is a violent attack that contributes to the triumph of destructiveness, passed down the generations, beyond the wildest dreams of the criminal gang who carried it out.

From connection and its catastrophic loss, good lord, deliver us.

In February 1974, a week before Dad died, I visit him in the intensive care coronary unit at the Queen Elizabeth Hospital Birmingham, following a second heart attack. He is sitting up in bed, looking frail. *Are you all right?* I say.

He points out his consultant, busy with a bevy of junior doctors, at another bed some distance away—telling me he asked the consultant whether he had been there with him when he nearly died. The consultant told him, kindly and honestly, I think, that he had not been there but had been kept in touch. I feel very moved remembering this last conversation with my father. I had been in touch at a distance with Dad for a very long time. At his graveside, I speak the words of committal

in sure and certain hope.

GOING NORTH

We set off for Carlisle in the Standard 8 at four o'clock in the dark. My father is organised with detailed AA maps of the journey that my mother uses to navigate. The most exciting moment is reaching Shap Fell. All eyes are on the needle of the temperature gauge as it moves clockwise towards the red. My father stops the car and lets the engine cool. We make it over the top.

My father writes every weekend with news to Hilda, his favourite sister. He is very particular about writing paper, always of a good quality, filling his fountain pen with Quink Royal Blue. I use Quink Permanent Black. We grow different from our mother and father but are chips off the old block.

Aunt Hilda and Uncle Carl and their two daughters live in a semi-detached house, larger than ours, facing a meadow running down to a distant line of trees behind which Burnstock Beck makes its way into the River Eden. Hilda is hugely energetic, organised, warm and friendly.

She unfailingly provides chips and home-made ice cream with our first evening meal, and a schedule worked out for us all to visit our cousins in Westmorland. Carl is a physics master at Carlisle Grammar School, a lovely man, and we enjoy him taking us to see his latest gadgets on the go in the garage.

My favourite visit is to Cousin Alex Glessal Fothergill, a sheep farmer from Brough Sowerby. The fell rearing up behind the family's farmhouse has an awesome beauty. Mum is a bit overawed by Hilda but she keeps her end up.

My father does not wear the Brylcreem that makes his hair flat and black when he goes to work. His hair is free and wavy and reddish. During the war, his mates called him Sandy. I tell him he should always wear his hair like that.

Mum loves Carl. When I was small, Dad was in Ceylon, she took me on the train to Carlisle to meet with Hilda and Carl. Carl is a keen amateur photographer and a picture of me, about one year old, sitting up, is in the dining room at Norman Avenue. My parents are happy together in father's country, on these holidays in Carlisle. I really have no doubt that their happiness was connected with a mysterious high fever that hits me for six and departs after two days or so as suddenly as it arrives. It happens on two successive visits. Back home, my mother takes me to Dr Dora who is concerned that it might be rheumatic fever and considers referring me for investigation. But there is no recurrence of fever, and the matter is dropped. It is a heart matter but of a different kind.

On these visits, Hilda would sometimes entertain us at supper with an oft-repeated story, told her by her aunt, Elizabeth Annie—mother of my sheep-farming cousin, Alex Glessal—about Elizabeth Annie's grandmother, Hellen Glessal. Elizabeth Annie told Hilda that Hellen Glessal was very particular, refusing to eat her porridge without a silver spoon—a tiny cameo that might suggest stubbornness, resentment, loss, and superiority. Hellen Glessal might have born on the wrong side of the bed sheets, as my aunt put it, of a Duke of Argyll. *La pièce de résistance* was the production of a copperplate letter dated Edinburgh, 2nd March, 1846, received by Hellen Glessal from the lawyers of the Marquis of Lorne, George Glassell Campbell—who later became 8th Duke of Argyll—as one of the Heirs of Entail to the Estate of Longniddry in the County of Haddington, North Britain. (Longniddry is a village 13 miles north-east of Edinburgh.) The letter states the Marquis to be the heir in possession of the Estate of Longniddry under a Deed of Entail executed by his maternal grandfather, the late John Glassell, Esq. of Longniddry. It seeks the signatures of the Heirs of Entail to back an application to Parliament for authority to make certain changes to the Estate that would be financially advantageous to George Glassell Campbell and future heirs. (The number 77 at the top left-hand corner of the letter indicates that "Hellen Glassell" is well down the list of the Heirs of Entail!)

POST
Collage
(1994-1995)
Anthony Whishaw

I am all ears. I imagine turning the tables on that bastarding bastard Mr Cook, a teacher at High Street Harborne Junior School, who enjoyed raising a laugh from the class about my middle name, Glessal.

I do not know that hidden in the telling of this family romance is a haunting experience of connection and its catastrophic loss. During my childhood, I never hear her name spoken. Dad's funeral releases my mum from her silence. She tells me that Dad's mother was called Mary Eleanor. She killed herself. Once, Mum says, Dad talked to her about Mary Eleanor, but became so upset and distressed that she thought it best not to talk about her with him again.

From connection and its catastrophic loss, good lord, deliver us.

Mary Eleanor Cook Robinson, born 13th October, 1877, and my grandfather, James Alexander McCraken Millar, born 1st October, 1874, were married on 3rd September, 1901 at the Primitive Methodist Chapel, Cecil Street, Carlisle. James Millar was a railway clerk at Carlisle for the London North-West Railway (LNW), and Mary Eleanor's father, John Robinson, was a locomotive fireman.

My dad, Charles William, born on 18th March, 1914, four months before the outbreak of the Great War, was named after Mary Eleanor's oldest brother. His sisters each received one of their mother's names—Mary Hilda born on 24th November, 1905, and her older sister, Eleanor May on 1st May, 1903.

Studio wedding photo of James and Mary Eleanor, 1901

My grandfather James died on 6th July, 1917 from pneumonia, aged 42 years, nine months, and five days, when Mary Eleanor was 39 years, eight months and 25 days, my father three years, three months, and 19 days, Aunt Hilda 11 years, seven months and 12 days, and Aunt May 14 years, two months and five days.

When James died, the family moved to live with Mary Eleanor's mother, Martha Ann Robinson at 3 Lismore Street, Carlisle. Martha Ann, Mum tells me, with unusually strong feelings, was a depressed, difficult woman, an unpleasant bully who made the family's life a misery before she died in 1924. Six years after her death, Mary Eleanor died on 3rd May, 1930 from coal gas poisoning in the kitchen of 3 Lismore Street. Hilda found her body in the morning. Her death certificate reads suicide while temporarily insane—the coroner's verdict of "temporarily insane" a kindness to the family. It is very sad. I do not know any more.

The summer after Dad died, I am very preoccupied with his origins. Aunt Hilda has a little red notebook in which, when she was young, she had written down information given her by her aunt, Elizabeth Annie Millar. Hilda kindly lends me the notebook.

In (Sweetheart) New Abbey, Dumfries is the tombstone of Hellen Glessall and her husband William Miller, and two of their children

> In Memory of
> Wm. Millar who died at
> Shawhead 1859 age 78 years
> Also
> Rbt. Miller his son who died
> At Whitehall 1824
> Aged 16 years
> Also
> Elizabeth Millar daughter of
> Wm. Millar who died at
> Shawhead 27 Aug 1861
> Aged 53 years
> Also, Hellen Glessall wife of
> Wm Miller who died
> Shawhead 3 June 1864
> Aged 79 years

Hellen Glessal/Glessall and William Millar had nine children. Robert Millar, my great-grandfather, is a late last child (b. 5th January, 1830 d. 1909 (78yrs)).

Robert Millar married 6th Dec, 1861 Rachel Reid (b. 17th Jan, 1836, daughter of Wm Reid & Catherine McKie). Robert and Rachel had seven children.

Wm. Glassel Millar b. 29th March, 1863 Registered at New Abbey Dumfries,

Baptised Shawhead, New Abbey by Rev Dudgion, Dalbeattie. d. at Glasgow 30th Aug, 1913

Margaret Millar b. 17th June, 1866 Registered at Bolton, Westmorland. Bap.

Bewley Castle by Rev. Tanniehill U.P minister Penrith.

Catherine Jane Millar b. 23rd April, 1868

Robt. Glessal Millar b. 19th Oct, 1869

d. 20th Jan, 1870 (Bronchitis—Interred at Bolton)

Hellen Glessal Millar b. 12th Dec, 1870

James Alexander McCraken Millar b. 1st Oct, 1874 Bap. at Bolton Chapel by Rev. Kains, F.M. Appleby minister. d. 6th July, 1917. Interred Upperby, Carlisle

Elizabeth Annie Millar b. 10th May, 1877 Registered Morland. Bap. at Morland
By Rev. J. Knight, Vicar

Robert Millar

Rachel Reid

A year after Hellen Glessal died, Robert Millar with Rachel, his wife, and their first child, left Dumfries for Bolton, a Westmoreland village, in the Eden valley, with the Pennines on one side and the Lake District on the other. He left, reports the red notebook, with James McCraken, described as a gentleman farmer, to work as a bailiff on the Bewley Castle estate. The estate, at that time, belonged to the Bishops of Carlisle. James McCraken must have had a lease as a tenant farmer. At Bolton, five children were born to Robert and Rachel, the last being my grandfather James. Rachel became almost blind owing to the reeky house.

The notebook narrates something striking. After ten years at Bewley Castle, James McCraken goes bankrupt, disappears from view as abruptly as he appears in the first place. The odd thing, made odder by the lack of any comment, is that this is the same year that James, my grandfather, is born and baptised James McCraken. Elizabeth Annie, James' favourite younger sister—my aunt Hilda's source of information—possibly knew more, but if so, she is keeping mum.

What is not speculation is that the family's move from Bolton to the nearby estate of Crossrigg Hall, where James was a bailiff for 20 years, worked out well. While much smaller these days, it remains a smart, well-run estate. Robert and Rachel with their family, including James my grandfather, and Elizabeth Annie, the source of the information in the red notebook who was born there, lived in Eddy House, a large, attractive cottage just outside the pretty village of Morden.

The village schoolmaster took an interest in James, and placed him for an exam at Lancaster, which got him onto the railways. Leaving home at 15 years old, he worked first at Peterborough and then at Carlisle LNWR goods office where he became chief clerk.

James with Elizabeth Annie—his favourite younger sister

born at Morland

I discover to my great surprise from the red notebook that the person I knew as Uncle Harold was Mary Eleanor's second eldest brother, Harold Robinson, b. 1878—a great uncle to me and brother to my dad's dead mum. As a young teenager, I met Harold, then in his seventies, long retired from his job at the Annan Gas Company, nationalised in 1949, where he had done well for himself—or so I pick up from my parents' talk when he comes to stay for a weekend. As in my visits, there is no mention of Mary Eleanor. I notice that Dad is very deferential to Harold, a stout, friendly person. One afternoon, Harold takes us, my parents, my brother and myself, out to tea in a hotel in the country and asks what we would like. I pipe up immediately with a request for chicken sandwiches, as good a treat as it gets in those days, getting daggers looks from my parents. Uncle Harold laughs and does not disappoint.

Looking back, it feels likely that Dad supressed feelings of anger and resentment that his family had not made some arrangement that could have allowed him to stay at Carlisle Grammar School and continue his education. The family valued education and both his sisters married teachers. But the loss of his schooling would have been so overshadowed by the death of his mum and his vulnerability.

One evening, the week following Trinity Sunday 1969, when I am ordained priest, I celebrate my first Eucharist at Pershore Abbey, Worcestershire, where I serve my title as a curate. Mum and Dad come. As the church empties, people going over the road for refreshments, Dad stays behind. I sense his increasing frailty and I think it frightens me. He is tearful and hugs me and says how moved he felt when I gave red roses to Mum at the end of the service. I felt embarrassed at him being so emotional, and enrobed in my specialness, I am a bit rejecting.

Reflecting on it, I think that Dad's experience of me giving the red roses to my mum felt reparative for him. I think me giving the flowers to Mum stirred his ancient pain and helplessness with his mum, who became so severely depressed. What I mean is that I am imagining his own subjective experience of connection and its catastrophic loss, with a catastrophic belief that he had made her depressed by killing his father. His father died when he was just three and a quarter, at the height of the Oedipal situation, with its intense rivalry.

Such a lot that Dad and I were not able to talk about, together but, talking with him in the conversation I am having here now, I imagine him reminding me of what he said to me in his letter to me on my first birthday.

You see in the little family you
belong to we always send a letter

to each other on birthdays,
just to say how much we love them,
for sometimes we don't always say
all those nice things to each
other that we ought to: so just
in case we have forgotten anything
we send this special letter.

*From connection and its catastrophic loss, good lord,
deliver us.*

The red notebook leaves me in the dark about the
relationship between Hellen Glessal/Glassell and John
Glassell, Esq. of Longniddry, maternal grandfather to
George Glassell Campbell. What was the relationship that
made her an Heir of Entail of the Longniddry estate, albeit
well down the line? I need to find out the names of Hellen
Glessal's parents. In Scotland, at that time, old registers of
deaths were kept in the home of the local Registrar.

I am very high in these summer months after Dad dies.
The goddess points north and rises up, flying up the M6
to Carlisle, then up to Gretna, east through Annan, the
Solway Firth to the south, and dropping down to New
Abbey, Dumfries. There I find the name of the local
Registrar, a Mrs Murray who lives close to New Abbey.
Mrs Murray is most helpful and welcoming. I am able to

find the two entries I am looking for in the 1855 Register of Deaths in the Parish of New Abbey, The Stewartry of Kirkcudbright.

Millar	Died	Age	Parents	Informant
William.	1859	78yrs	William Millar	William
Labourer	25th April		Farmer	Millar
Married	Shawhead		Son	
	New Abbey		Elizabeth Millar	
			Maiden name	
			Maxwell	

Elen	Died	Age	Parents	Informant
Millar	3rd June	76yrs	Robert Glessle	Robert
Widow to	1864		Farmer	Millar
William				
Millar				
Shawhead				
Labourer	New Abbey		Janet Glessle	
			Maiden surname	
			Glessle	

The register entry is solid evidence that Hellen Glessal/ Hellen Glassell/Elen Glessle Millar's parents were Robert Glessle and Janet Glessle from Shawhead, New Abbey.

There is nothing more to learn at New Abbey. But I cannot stop. The goddess rises up again, flying the A76 to Kilmarnock, past Glasgow, then the A82 along Loch Lomond and right up to Fort William. *How far are we going?* she says. *Until we can go no further,* I say. West to Mallaig, the landscape majestic and beautiful—the ferry to Skye, cross Skye to Uig, and the foot ferry to Tarbet, the Isle of Harris, the land of Harris Tweed.

Returning, the energy of a piece of music on the car radio seizes me. It is music I recognise but do not know what it is. When it gets to the end, I discover it is Felix Mendelssohn's *Hebrides'* overture, inspired by the noise of the sea at Fingal's Cave, on Staffa with its huge hexagonal basalt columns, molten lava forced up through the earth, crystallised by contact with the water. An EP of the *Hebrides'* overture is one of the first records I buy for that first Bush record player.

The names of Hellen Glessal's parents allow me to solve the genealogical puzzle. A catalogue search at London University Library brings up a well-documented genealogy, *Glessell of Scotland and Virginia* (1). It shows Hellen Glessal's father, Robert Glessle, was the youngest of three brothers, John, Andrew and Robert—the children of Robert Glassil, a farmer in the village of Roucan, near the village of Torthorwald, Dumfriesshire, and Mary Kelton, daughter of Matthew Kelton of Torthorwald. (Torthorwald is a Viking name; maybe the Glassil/Glessle/ Glessals descend from Vikings.)

Robert Glessle, the youngest brother of the marriage, marries his cousin, Janet Glassle, and inherits half the farm. Hellen Glessal (b. c. 1787) is the sixth of nine children from that marriage.

It is John, the oldest of the three brothers, who becomes John Glassell, Esq. of Longniddry, the maternal grandfather of George Glassell Campbell, the 8th Duke of Argyll (b. 30th April, 1823). The union of Scotland with England in 1707 opens up the British colonies, for ambitious young Scots. John Glassell leaves Scotland for Fredericksburg in the colony of Virginia. At the start of the American Revolutionary War (1775-1783), now a wealthy man, he purchases the estate of Longniddry in East Lothian, and marries Helen (born c. 1750), daughter of John Buchan of Letham. They have one living child, a daughter, Joan Glassell (b. Longniddry 1796).

John Glassell dies shortly before Joan's tenth birthday, and fourteen years later, 17th April, 1820, Joan, a young heiress, marries Lord John Campbell, young brother of the 6th Duke of Argyll. She dies 22nd January, 1828, from medical complications following the birth of her fourth child, a baby girl, who died. It is Joan Glassell's second son, George Glassell Campbell (b. 30th April, 1823), the Marquis of Lorne, who writes in 1846 to Hellen Glessal, as an heir of entail to the estate of Longniddry, a year before his accession as 8th Duke.

The Church of England, unlike Rome, does not do leaving Holy Orders. I make up a ritual, a journey to Cuddesdon where I leave my ordination stole, preaching scarf and surplice with the housekeeper at the vicarage for recycling. The college is on its summer holidays. I walk round the place, the old trees, the two croquet lawns, one impossibly sloping, the door to the common room unlocked as ever from the garden. I feel utterly bereft. Leaving the Church is not a decision I regret but it is so sad. I injure those I love, I lose many friends, I lose my family, I lose my home.

From connection and its catastrophic loss, good lord, deliver us.

Edna O'Brien's *The Little Red Chairs* ends:

'You would not believe how many words there are for *home* and what savage music there can be wrung from it.'

PD: (Introduction)... Her new novel takes its impulse from the butchery during the siege of Sarajevo, and the fact that the Serbian fugitive war criminal Radovan Karadzic was found living anonymously in Serbia as an alternative therapist.... The novel ends with the [migrant] women performing Shakespeare's Midsummer Night's Dream. *I asked her why she ends the novel with a reference to the savage music of home.*

EO'B: Well, home, the loss of home, the yearning for home, the search for home. Home as we know is many things. It can be a country, another person, a building in bricks and mortar, or an existential inner yearning. Or how to be at home in the world, full of danger, knife-edge existence and full of unknown as well… Each person would mobilize it differently… and the feeling for home, from the youngest child to the oldest person.

PD … I think it was Rilke who famously said, 'We are all unsaddled, we are not at home.' But for you, from the earliest books to the memoir to this, home is a very powerful itch that you need to scratch.

EO'B (sharply putting PD right) *I think it is more than an itch, a wound, and in* The Little Red Chairs *those who have been kicked out of their homes, or out of their countries, who were sent away and can't come back, or are wanderers of the world—I would think using the word in a wider sense there are more homeless people in the world than there are people in home.*

Edna O'Brien—as she publishes *The Little Red Chairs* (2016)—in conversation with Philip Dodd. BBC Radio 3.

One Christmas time, alone and depressed, I travel to Wales to spend Christmas Day with my mother. On Boxing

Day morning, as I am saying goodbye, Mum becomes convulsed with tears. She asks me if I would stay. It is the second time I see my mother cry. I hug her but leave as planned to spend Boxing Day with my cousin Pat. Leaving her by herself that day is something I so much regret.

It is a Wednesday evening. Bill phones to say that Pat is very ill. She is dying of cancer. He says he knows we are close and that she will want to see me. I am going abroad to teach on the Friday until the Sunday. I am restricted in my thinking, enrobed in a new specialness of psychoanalysis, that I do not see what I need to do, and what Pat wants me to do. I tell Bill I will come on Monday. Pat dies on the Sunday.

At the funeral, I learn that during the week before Pat died, she was very upset and angry at being hit by her mother as a child. I so much regret that I did not go straight up to Birmingham to see her, to climb those stairs to Pat, and share those things we could have shared, and then leave.

To live in current reality means having to face, against our will, the need to recognise and mourn what is lost and gone forever, our accumulated feelings of loss and deprivation and the painful feelings of sadness they bring and how that has come about. Only then can we mourn and do all that we can to repair the damage.

Jim gets up from his red cushion, stretches himself and stands with his paws against my knee. I reach down and pick him up and put him on my lap.

Detour

It was from Point Comfort in Virginia in 1619 that America's first African slaves came off the slave ships. Tobacco was Virginia's chief export, with demand from England and Europe, a labour-intensive crop. By the 1750s there were 145,000 slaves in the Chesapeake Bay Region (2). The wealth of John Glassell, and his brother Andrew Glassell who followed him to Virginia, was built on the back of the Atlantic slave trade.

In *From Roucan to Riches, The Rise of the Glassell Family,* David McKenzie Robertson (3) presents a letter dated Fredericksburg July 13th 1765 from John Glassell—29 years old, having been in Virginia for around 10 years—to his brother Andrew after the death of their father. "He has left us," John writes at the beginning of the letter, "to mourn an affectionate father." At the close of the letter John writes: "I am every day sinking a property in the Country and it requires all my attention. I wish you and my brother [Robert] were both here. I could soon settle you on a good tract of land, and with your money purchase negroes to labour for you; and your fortunes, with half the industry you use, would increase much faster. However, I don't mean to persuade you to anything contrary to your inclination, only I should be glad you were near me that my influence might be of service to you. Let me hear from you frequently. Remember me to my uncle, brother, and all friends" (pp. 35-37).

Unlike their brother Robert, Andrew did join John in Virginia and, unlike his loyalist brother, did not return to England but "became sole owner of the Glassell plantation in Madison County, paying John the full value of the property after the peace settlement" (p.254).

The origins of John Glassell's wealth in the slave trade had become gentrified through his purchase of the Longniddry estate and his marriage to Helen Buchan, some 40 years before his daughter Joan Glassell married Lord John Campbell. However, the toxic culture and attitudes of the violent rape of black African people is not so easily laundered. It is likely to be passed down through the generations and a possible factor in Joan's son, George Glassell Campbell, the 8th Duke's infamous tyranny in the later clearances from the lands of Western Highlands and in particular the south-west, the Ross of Mull, the poorest part of this most beautiful of the Western Isles. The Scottish historian T M Devine (4) has written a balanced account of the complex history of *The Scottish Clearances: A History of the Dispossessed 1600-1900.* He writes:

...even before the potatoes failed in 1846, the 8th Duke of Argyll and his managers had determined by 1840 to carry out large-scale removals on the Ross [of Mull] and [the island of] Tiree of crofters and cottars and replace them with medium-sized mixed farms and extensive sheep runs which would be mainly rented by Islay kinsmen and associates of his factor, John Campbell [John Campbell of Ardmore, Chamberlain of the Duke of Argyll's lands in Tiree and the Ross of Mull] (p. 327).

In large part it was the clearances of the later famine period that marked out the experience of the western Highlands and Islands as different from the history of dispossession in the rest of Scotland. These removals were unleashed against communities still suffering from the ravages of a major destitution crisis. They affected many on the Hebridean islands, were concentrated in both time and space and for the most part designed to drive out the poorest families and the "redundant population". Several were enforced by draconian means with little concern for humanity or the welfare of the people. Racialist assumptions undeniably helped to fashion those responsible for the strategy of dispossession. (p. 331).

BORN OF DAVID'S LINE

The Adoration of the Kings in the Snow, 1563, by the Flemish painter Pieter Bruegel the Elder (1525-1569)—an oil on oak panel 35 x 55 cm in the Oskar Reinhart Collection 'Am Römerholz', Winterthur—is painted in a precarious present, just before the Netherlands' revolt against the tyranny of the Hapsburg Spanish empire, and the ensuing Eighty Years' War (which ended with a division between the new Protestant Dutch Republic in the north and a Catholic south).

The art critic Joseph Leo Koerner (1) writes:

In a gesture of sublime irony, the painter makes the biblical Epiphany—Christ's singular World is changing, "coming to light"—almost disappear. Tiny, at the lower left of this painting, the sacred actors recede into the shadows of the ruined stables. It takes work to make them out: the Magi, Joseph and the Virgin and Child—the lattermost group so close to the framing edge that they almost escape the picture.

The African Magus stands, as usual, a step back from the threshold, his features merging with the background darkness that the brilliant snow punctuates and obscures. Bruegel knew that his art departed from religion. Supreme artistic self-consciousness allows his works to be their own best commentary. Here the eclipse of biblical narrative is not some career choice he has made—say, to follow the

116

dictates of contemporary taste or to give an alibi for painting landscape. It is, rather, the true state of things, both back then, when Christ was born, homeless and uncelebrated, in a stable in Bethlehem, and now, in the painter's age, in the Flemish lifeworld Bruegel intimately knows and into which he projects Christ's birth.

…

Lead white comes to behave like snow, concealing what it touches. Observe in the picture the many boards and planks gathering snow rather as Bruegel's own panel gets coated in white….

This snow looks as if it will continue unabated, however, and if it does—the picture suggests—the Epiphany, both the one Bruegel paints, and his painting itself, will completely disappear.

Joseph Leo Koerner, *Bosch and Bruegel: From Enemy Painting to Everyday Life (2016)*. Princeton University Press: Princeton and Oxford (p. 284—286).

The connection between the ancestors and the gods, which promise protection and demand to be placated, was a theme in *Ancestors, Beyond Belief*, Radio 4, 29th May, 2017 presented by Ernie Rea. Julian Thomas, Professor of Archaeology at Manchester University tells a story about the period he is interested in that started around 4000BC when a change took place in the importance of ancestors.

After nomadic hunters and gatherers stopped moving around, the way that they looked at the world changed.

Julian Thomas said that, previously, hunters and gatherers tended for the most part to have an idea of ancestors out there in the landscape—so the ancestors may be in the forest, they may be ancestral presences. However, once people started to get domesticated plants and animals that they wanted to keep inside their community, they began to have lineages or clans or tribes that were collective owners of property. Their relationship to the ancestors is then very different because the ancestors are the house ancestors, the originators of a particular community. The ancestors are the people who cleared the waste, they are the people who opened up the pasture.

Ernie Rea asks whether these ancestors were gods? Julian Thomas says that they were certainly venerated but *venerate* is not perhaps the same thing as *worship*, and it may be that later on, moving towards the end of the Neolithic and the beginnings of the bronze age, some of these ancestors are converted into gods. The people see them as very active in the community. The gods are bestowers of blessings, they are sources of fertility, they are people who you have to propitiate in a whole series of ways.

When some ancestors are converted into gods, something really striking happens. In Mesopotamia, to the east of the Levantine region, and also Egypt, there emerge rulers, kings of city states, who build huge, impressive buildings. A city-state like Babylon or Ashur/Assyria evolves its own particular pantheon of gods, with a chief deity, promising protection, with particular characteristics and history.

Where a city-state rises to power, becoming the centre of an empire, subjugating other city-states, or is defeated by another city-state, these events are believed to be inseparable from the activity of the gods and the necessity for them to be propitiated. And only one man, the king, the chosen one of the deity, is believed to possess the power that can ensure that the deity is propitiated, and that the city-state will receive his favour and protection.

With the capture of the city of Jerusalem by David, the phenomenon of rival gods that promise blessings and having to be propitiated enters the bible story centre stage for a second time—the first time being the fight between the gods of Egypt and the God of some Israelite tribes who have fallen into slavery.

The work of Robert Alter (3) *The David Story* has recently shown me the complexity of the biblical story of David, which, like *The Iliad*, bears the marks of the mind of an extraordinary storyteller. The story begins with David as a special person inhabiting a world with only two positions—triumph or humiliation—who becomes king, chosen by the deity, before pivoting around loss and mourning to show him living in a world where vulnerability, mortality, weakness, and bonds of love and attachment exist in conflict with the longing for power. Robert Alter writes:

> He begins as the fair-haired boy of Israel.... Everyone seems to love him. He is beautiful, he is musical, and he is brave and brilliantly resourceful on the battlefield. He is also, from the start, quite calculating, and it can scarcely be an accident that until the midpoint of his story every one of his utterances, without exception, is made on a public occasion and arguably is contrived to serve his political interests.... Beset by mortal dangers, David is constantly prepared to do almost anything in order to survive.... profiting politically from the chain of violent deaths in the house of Saul while vehemently dissociating himself from each of the killings....
>
> And yet, David is more than a probing representation of the ambiguities of political power. He is also an affecting and troubling image of human destiny as husband and father and as a man moving from youth to prime to the decrepitude of old age. The great pivotal moment of the whole story in this regard is when he turns to his perplexed courtiers, after putting aside the trappings of mourning he had assumed for his ailing infant son, now dead, and says, "I am going to him. He will not come back to me." These are the very first words David pronounces that have no conceivable political motive, that give us a glimpse into his inwardness, revealing

his sense of naked vulnerability to the inexorable mortality that is the fate of all humankind. For the rest of the story, we see David's weakness and his bonds of intimate attachment in fluctuating conflict with the imperatives of power that drive him as a king surrounded by potential enemies and betrayers.

I first become acquainted with, and fascinated by the David story much earlier, from a different angle, with my Old Testament supervisions with John Bowker at Cambridge in the mid-'60s. I learn how David becomes king of a city-state. He makes it to the top.

The Israelite confederation begins as a group of tribes and clans with disparate origins and history, but the group develops a collective belief in the shape of a covenant with their God. Tied into the covenant is a saving history in which the disparate tribes and clans making up the confederation are saved as a people by their God from the tyranny of being enslaved in the empire of Egypt and its pharaohs.

David is a military leader from the southern tribe of Judah. His forces capture Jerusalem, a fortified southern city not previously occupied by any of the Israelite tribes. It is highly probable that, when captured, Jerusalem, like Babylon, has a tradition of kingship that links the king closely to the gods (2). The Jerusalem tradition includes El Elyon, God most high, chief deity, who dwells on

Mount Zion and is linked to ownership of the surrounding land.

David and his court engineer—not without opposition—the incorporation of El Elyon and Jerusalem's tradition into the confederation's covenant belief. There is little doubt that, as king, David is closely linked to God, as we see in the association between king and God in the psalms. For example, Psalm 45 suggests that on this occasion of a royal wedding, the king is addressed as God:

Your throne, O God, endures for ever and ever,
Your royal sceptre is a sceptre of equity

Under David, and his son Solomon, Jerusalem becomes the capital of an empire, with conquest and coercion of other groups and peoples. Things were on a roll, the glory years of Jerusalem, resources moving from the periphery to the centre.

How excellent thy name, O Lord
in all the world is known.

However, there follows a slow falling. After the death of Solomon, the northern tribes in the confederation break away from the control of the Jerusalem court, setting up a rival kingdom of Israel in the north, with its own court in its capital, Samaria. Other empires emerge to triumph, and to be humiliated, in their turn.

A newly ascendant and threatening Assyria (geographically speaking, roughly modern-day Iraq), with its capital, Nineveh, expands to become a huge empire (c. 911- 609 BC). It is a massive threat. Deportation, coupled with communal forced settlement, is employed on a massive scale; systematically applied to conquered areas (4).

From connection and its catastrophic loss, good lord, deliver us.

Amos, a prophet from the north, Israel, makes an original interpretation of the growing threat of invasion by Assyria, of the loss of the people's land and recognisable identity around the covenant. Prophets have been very critical before, as in earlier criticisms of David's behaviour. But Amos is the first to interpret the threatened invasion and occupation by Assyria as signalling the end of the covenant. God had given up on them, taken himself away, retribution for the people's failure to propitiate him. They have become insignificant.

You only have I known of all the families of the earth;
Therefore, I will punish you for all your iniquities
(Amos 3.2).

Prophecies, like dreams, come from the psyche. I think that in ancient Israel we see a pattern similar to that seen in a boy from Birmingham—of a subjective experience of connection and its catastrophic loss, with an underlying, catastrophic belief that he has damaged a connecting door to goodness, bringing unbearable guilt and threatening collapse.

The Assyrian empire, their own gods demanding propitiation, extract in turn heavy tribute payments from the Levantine kingdoms. Some, like the Phoenicians, adapt successfully to the changed political situation, transforming their coastal Mediterranean cities into profitable ports. But it brings the end for the northern kingdom of Israel. Israel is seen and treated in reality as a people that has no right to exist. In 721 BC, Samaria is invaded, captured and its people dispersed.

Next, Assyria falls in turn to the war machine of a newly ascendant neo-Babylonian empire. In the south, the melancholic prophet Jeremiah interprets the threat of invasion by Babylon's armies along the same lines as Amos' preaching earlier in the north.

And in 587 BC, an army of the Babylonian empire invades the southern kingdom of Judah, sacks Jerusalem and deports its elite to exile in Babylon. Judah is seen and treated in reality as a people that has no right to exist.

With the rise of the Persian Empire, which in turn takes down the Babylonians, King Cyrus makes a political decision to allow all the different peoples deported by the Babylonians to return to their homelands if they wished. We do not know what proportion of Judeans, Jews, return from exile to Jerusalem—but those who do come back to a ruined city. Many Jews become part of the growing Jewish diaspora, which later spreads further after the Roman invasion 67 AD and destruction of Jerusalem.

The only evidence we have of the return to Jerusalem (other than the independent evidence of Cyrus's decree allowing all captives to return home) is the internal evidence of the Old Testament that, as we have it now, is a post-exilic revision of older written and oral sources. Moreover, this post-exilic revision is by southern editors. And, as I explain below, the southern redactors are in no sense a neutral party.

The internal evidence strongly suggests that after the return, there are tightening measures—traditions codified, religious authority figures reinforced, and foremost a hardened stance to the wrongness of marriage to foreigners. The tightening measures are intended to ensure that God is propitiated correctly. We just do not know the variety of factors that may have contributed to this stance against exogamy. If one knew the actual history—and there is no independent source of evidence—the picture would probably be extremely complex, with a diversity of social, economic and political factors contributing to the hardened stance to the wrongness of marriage to foreigners.

The southern editors' view is similar to both the northern prophet Amos and the southern prophet Jeremiah—but with a difference. The position is hardened. There is really no doubt that the editors believe that it is first and foremost the intermarriage with foreigners that led to God's retribution, to the invasions, the loss of the land, and the exile.

Moreover, the southern editors are not neutral. They blame near-foreigners, the northerners, the Samaritans, for intermarriage with foreigners. The message the redactors preach to their group, the Jews/Judeans, following the return, is: *If you don't want a repeat of connection and its catastrophic loss, if you don't want to be cut off from goodness, to be insignificant, do not inter-marry with foreigners.* And the Samaritans are seen as beyond the pale.

This hardening is a shift away from the pre-exilic story of David, of a world of vulnerability, mortality, weakness, where bonds of love and attachment exist in conflict with the longing for power. John Bowker had a scholarly interest in the post-exilic period, but, in the undergraduate teaching of the Cambridge Divinity School of the middle-'60s, the period did not get much attention. The message was pretty clear, *Get off the Old Testament bus here, and pick up the connecting New Testament bus.*

The message was welcome to me. Reading theology at the Cambridge Divinity School, I felt the post-exilic period very boring. I was missing something big. However, one person, from a foreign (non-theological) discipline, got hold of what was going on. In the mid-'90s, as I have said before, Elizabeth Spillius drew my attention to the work of the social anthropologist Edmund Leach (5). I discover that, back in the 1960s, Edmund Leach put forward a hypothetical new concept, that he calls the "post-exilic myth". He contends that the southern editors' redaction of the biblical stories—following invasion, loss and exile— was very radical indeed. The text of the body of the Old Testament as a whole, as we have it now, writes Leach (1969):

> asserts that the Jewish political title to the land of Palestine is a direct gift from God to the descendants of Israel (Jacob). This provides the fundamental basis for Jewish endogamy— the Jews should be a people of pure blood and pure religion, living in isolation in their promised land (p. 31).

This assertion, through the body of the Old Testament as a whole, is what Leach calls the post-exilic myth. He is using the idea of myth in a specific way. Following Claude Lévi-Strauss, Leach terms the post-exilic redaction a myth in the sense that it mediates a major "structural contradiction (large scale incompatibility of intention)".

> The problem is not resolved because it is irresolvable; yet it seems to be resolved ... Myths serve to provide an apparent resolution, or "mediation" of problems which are by their v e r y nature incapable of any final resolution (Leach, 1969, p.54).

Leach argues that the structural contradiction mediated by the post-exilic myth covers up an irresolvable contradiction that everyone knows about. There is the post-exilic stance of maintaining the practice of endogamy and the purity of the faith. But the pre-exilic stories—known to everyone—are evidence of

> a less idealized form of tradition which represents the population of ancient Palestine as a mixture of many peoples over whom the Jews have asserted political dominance by right of conquest. The Jews and their "foreign" neighbours intermarry freely (p. 31).

Leach writes,

> there is total incompatibility between a rule of endogamy and the recognition that society consists of potentially antagonistic groups allied by marriage (p. 55).

Let me give a sense of how Edmund Leach tests his new concept, where the southern editors' work seeks to eradicate the irresolvable contradiction, where it conceals, like Bruegel's snow, what it touches.

Leach contends that a technique of analysis of the biblical texts using a variation of Lévi-Strauss's procedure for structural analysis demonstrates a systematic *structural* contradiction in the Biblical texts. He describes how, "in the Biblical texts this fundamental contradiction is glossed over by [the editors] offering repeated partial, but contradictory, solutions" (p. 54). He describes how such repetitious " 'variations on a theme' which constantly recur in mythological systems serve to blur the edges of... 'contradictions' and remove them from immediate consciousness" (p.39). Leach uses a variation of structural analysis to show that "in a formal sense the [redacted] Biblical texts consistently affirm the righteousness of endogamy and the sinfulness of exogamy, but the structural message keeps harking back to the contradiction" (p. 39).

Leach gives a detailed demonstration of how pre-exilic stories are penetrated by disinformation from the Biblical texts surrounding the legitimacy of Solomon's kingship. He shows that here, as elsewhere in the Biblical texts, editorial work draws the reader away from evidential inconsistencies to post-exilic dogma—steering attention to the point of view the redactors want to propagate. That the prominent southern ancestor figure, King Solomon, took foreign wives is well-known; pre-exilic stories of his foreign marriages are much too well-known among people for the editors to get rid of them. Leach shows how the work of editorial synthesis persuades the reader that Solomon's marriages to foreign women actually exemplify the righteousness of endogamy.

Leach argues that this examination of the Old Testament, using the techniques of structural analysis—showing an irresolvable contradiction *behind* the formal message of the post-exilic stance of maintaining the practice of endogamy and the purity of the faith—makes it very probable that the message of the "overriding virtue of close kin endogamy" with its great interest in showing the descent of important Biblical figures from Abraham and the promise of the land is essentially the work of the post-exilic redactors.

Henri Poincaré (6), writing about mathematical discovery, says that, "among the combinations we choose, the most fruitful are often those which are formed of elements borrowed from widely separated domains (p. 51)". Leach's hypothesis of the post-exilic myth is an example of such fruitful discovery, crossing different conceptual domains—where Leach's use of a variation of Lévi-Strauss's procedure for structural analysis penetrates the Old Testament stories. The result is a new way of seeing the bible story. However, Leach left his hypothesis of the post-exilic myth there; he did not develop it further.

After Elizabeth Spillius drew my attention to Leach's discovery, it rattled around for years in my mind, getting inside my internal model of psychoanalysis to crystallise as the idea that I call hardened myth (7). This notion gives a new portal to look at the world of the relationship between the Jewish and Christian groups down the centuries within the Western tradition.

I have described above the emergence of the post-exilic myth as a defining shift in the development of Judaism; a crisis of identity coming from experience of connection and its catastrophic loss. The execution of Jesus by the occupying Roman power is also an experience of connection and catastrophic loss, bringing a crisis of identity and a shift in the development of Christianity.

What I call the Jesus myth in the Christian tradition, and Leach's hypothesis of the post-exilic myth in the Jewish tradition are idealised paranoid belief systems, that I call hardened myth, which cover up, keep out of consciousness, an underlying catastrophic belief of damage to a connecting door to goodness, with unbearable guilt—threatening collapse. Each belief system maps metaphorically onto the other—laying claim to exclusive access to salvation, a special people, a special church, and projection of vulnerability and damage into a near-foreign group.

In the post-exilic myth, the Jewish group triumph over the northern group. The group claims a privileged identity; the true inheritor of a promise made by God to Abraham and his descendants. God is propitiated by the practice of endogamy. Exclusive possession of goodness and virtue is asserted for the group; guilt, worthlessness, badness, inferiority, and fallibility are split off and projected into a near-foreign group, the Samaritans, humiliated and blamed for catastrophic loss with virtuous hatred.

In the Jesus myth, the new Christian group, that also claims to be born of David's line, triumphs over the Jewish group. Stealing its books, the Christian group claims a privileged identity; the true inheritors of a promise made by God to Abraham and his descendants. In the Jesus myth, God is propitiated and reconciled to human badness only through Jesus' submission to torture and death by crucifixion—the acceptance of the propitiation proven by a triumphant concrete resurrection. Exclusive possession of goodness and virtue is asserted for the Christian group; guilt, worthlessness, badness, inferiority, and fallibility are split off and projected into a near-foreign group, the Jews, humiliated and blamed for catastrophic loss with virtuous hatred.

Groups of all kinds—religious, psychoanalytic, political, scientific and artistic groups and so on—usually seek to control the transmission of their ideas and conventions.

But in hardened myth, vulnerability, damage and blame for catastrophic loss are projected into another group, whose own recognisable identity is devalued.

On 10th January, 381, this direction of travel becomes set in political, economic and social stone when the Spaniard Theodosius, emperor in the east, with his eye on the crumbling west, enforces doctrinal unity on the divided, arguing Christians. He issues an edict that proclaims the orthodoxy of the Trinitarian Nicene faith alone, and forbids heretics, that is to say anyone who thought differently, from assembling (8).

This closing of minds is not just an ordinary wish of a group to preserve the transmission of its own ideas. It is an attack on independent thinking—on a connecting door to goodness where one thing may get into another thing to create something new—harnessed to the power and violence of the state. It is a tyrannical underbelly of the continuity of collective Christian belief in the west that lasted over very many centuries.

Walking to Gallerie dell'Academia di Venezia

Human ingenuity and imagination, put to a variety of ends, are nevertheless also always part of the scene, but vulnerable to a tyrannical system because they emerge from independent thinking.

In a famous example of heresy hunting, Paolo Veronese appears before the Inquisition in Venice in July 1573. His painting of the *Last Supper*—a faded print of which from Gallerie dell'Academia di Venezia hangs in the hall of my house—has attracted the attention of the Inquisition. What attracts this attention is not some new religious group or religious idea but the sheer existence of independent thinking, in this case through the medium of painting. In the painting we see about fifty figures.

Other than Jesus and the twelve disciples, these include two German soldiers in armour, a clown with a parrot on his arm, two dwarfs, a man with a nosebleed, and in the foreground, a large dog. The viewer—whether excited by or hostile to its newness—recognises straightaway that these figures are not add-ons. Veronese's painting disturbs the Inquisition but also makes it problematic for them to use their usual instruments to control the transmission of ideas. Like Pieter Bruegel the Elder, Veronese knows that his art departs from religion. He is aware of danger. Asked by the Inquisition what the picture is intended to represent, Veronese replies, "It is a picture of the Last Supper, taken by Jesus with his Apostles in the house of Simon." John Bowker (9) points out, "the reply is either very able or very ignorant, for there was, according to the Gospels, no such thing (p. 309)". Veronese's reply, having the fight he needs to have with a tyrannical system, is a very canny answer.

The medium of theatre has many faces, and one of them is inclusivity and diversity—work of perspiration and imagination to face a truth. There is a complex relationship between the writing of a play, and its production, perhaps many years after the death of the playwright. Director, players, others involved in the production, all may bring a new sensibility that can change what we see.

David Nirenberg (10) writes that in *The Merchant of Venice*:

> Shakespeare used Shylock to represent the controversies and crises posed by rapid economic and cultural transformation –among them, the legalization of lending at interest in 1571, the rise of mercantilism, changes in the laws of bond and contract, even the introduction of commercial theatre. How does a Christian society, taught for hundreds of years that moneylending is "Judaising", and that "action can rarely or never please God, and therefore no Christian should be a merchant," make sense of the world in which interest is legal, and a merchant can proudly claim to "to act for the commodity of his countrie"? These questions had nothing to do with the real Jews or Judaism, but Shylock provided Shakespeare and his contemporaries with the foil against which to determine, as Portia puts the problem in the courtroom scene, "which is the merchant here, and which the Jew?"

I remember the opening night of the production of *The Merchant of Venice* directed by Trevor Nunn on 17ᵗʰ June, 1999, in the small Cottesloe at the National Theatre. I feel in my gut the punches that the playwright does not pull; the arrogance of representatives of the Christian group *and* the Jewish group that pushes individuals and the Venetian state itself to the knife-edge. I think that the play has everything to do not only with economic and cultural change, as stated by David Nirenberg, but with the relationship between the Jewish group and the Christian group in the Elizabethan minds that Shakespeare intimately knows—and which exists in the minds of people for centuries before and centuries after. A play within a play of hardened myth, two mirroring ideologies, always there in the wings to invade, to disturb.

Things begin with the merchant Antonio's (David Bamber) melancholia, and Bassanio's (Alexander Hanson) wish to resolve his debts, find love, have it all, by winning Portia (Derbhle Crotty), a beautiful, intelligent heiress. To put on a show for Portia, Bassanio turns to his friend Antonio, who is so besotted with him that he can deny him nothing.

Antonio does not lose a chance to pour contempt into Shylock (Henry Goodman), a member of Venice's Jewish group. Shakespeare's text is unflinching about the tyranny of the Christian group towards the Jewish group. Antonio's venom penetrates and disturbs the audience. But tyrannical too is the hate and contempt of the Jewish group towards the Christian group. In the financial contract that Antonio sets up and agrees with Shylock, a known enemy—that his own heart shall be his bond—Antonio turns a blind eye to the danger. Antonio's melancholic besotted-ness impairs his judgement and capacity to weigh risk.

In Nunn's production, following the news that Antonio's richly loaded trading ship is wrecked on the

Goodwins, David Bamber plays the wrecked Antonio as a dispossessed refugee or political prisoner, who trails helplessly after Shylock, now increasingly arrogant, Nazi-like. And Shylock's determination to enact the bond between him and Antonio is yet further inflamed by his daughter Jessica's (Gabrielle Jourdan) elopement with Lorenzo (Daniel Evans), a Christian.

> IV.1 293
> Would any of the stock of Barabbas
> Had been her husband, rather than a Christian. (11)

When Shylock arrives at court, we the audience watch in identification with the Christian group's utmost horror and dismay at what Shylock brings—a workman's ordinary metal toolbox. He opens the box to take out a knife and a pair of weighing scales. There is really no doubt of Shylock's intention to take Antonio's life, and triumph over the Republic, under the rules of engagement of the law court.

> IV.1 86
> Bassanio
> For thy three thousand ducats here is six.
>
> Shylock
> If every ducat in six thousand ducats

Were in six parts and every part a ducat,
I would not draw them; I would have my bond.

Duke
How shalt thou hope for mercy, rendering none?

Shylock
What judgment shall I dread, doing no wrong?
You have among you many a purchased slave,
Which, like your asses and your dogs and mules,
You use in abject and in slavish parts,
Because you bought them: shall I say to you,
"Let them be free! Marry them to your heirs!
Why sweat they under burdens? Let their beds
Be made as soft as yours and let their palates
Be seasoned with such viands"? You will answer,
"The slaves are ours." So do I answer you,
The pound of flesh, which I demand of him,
Is dearly bought; 'tis mine and I will have it.
If you deny me, fie upon your law!
There is no force in the decrees of Venice.
I stand for judgment. Answer; shall I have it? (11)

Amid this horror and dismay at the Venetian Court,
Portia, dressed as a man like a Doctor of Laws, appeals to
Shylock to show mercy. Her eloquence moves Shylock. He
hesitates, his conscience is stirred, but the moment passes.

Portia tells Antonio he must lay bare his bosom for the knife. But Portia has a plan for reparation. By combination of feminine and masculine, cunning, and sheer theatrical device, Portia effectively intervenes with a thought-through strategy.

> Portia
>
> A pound of that same merchant's flesh is thine,
> The court awards it, and the law doth give it.
>
> Shylock
> Most rightful judge!
>
> Portia
> And you must this flesh from off his breast,
> The law allows it and the Court awards it.
>
> Shylock
> Most learned judge! A sentence! Come, prepare!
>
> Portia
> Tarry a little, there is something else.
> This bond doth give thee here no jot of blood;
> The words expressly are a pound of flesh. (11)

Shylock is judged guilty "by direct or indirect attempts" of seeking the life of Antonio, a citizen of Venice. Antonio's life is saved, and so is the public face of the Republic. But then, after this rescue of the merchant Antonio, a transient reparative moment, the world of the wheel of triumph or humiliation turns again. There is no shortage of nastiness and cruelty and triumphing over Shylock. Asked by Portia what mercy Antonio can render Shylock, Antonio asks the presiding Duke (David Burt) and Court that Shylock become a Christian. The duke coerces Shylock to agree at pain of death.

But then, in this play there is a moment when something different happens. There is a small shift away from a world of just two positions—triumph or humiliation. Antonio asks the Duke and the Court to quit Shylock's fine of one half of his goods to the state, asking instead that Shylock sign a deed of gift of all he possesses *when he dies* "unto his son Lorenzo and his daughter". And regarding the other half of Shylock's goods due to him as the injured party, he asks the Court that the goods be held by him, and to go to Lorenzo and Jessica after Shylock's death.

That is to say, Antonio uses his position in the immediate present to ask the Court to modify its decision so as not to ruin Shylock financially and to ensure that Lorenzo (Christian) and Jessica (Jewish) inherit a substantial amount of money after Shylock's death.

In the audience, I feel it is a moment where Antonio, who nearly lost his life, and created a huge mess and near-disaster for his friends, pauses to reflect. A moment of depression, guilt feelings and reparative wishes, like a coming down following the excitement and destructiveness of war.

Now, it is true that this same act of reparation rubs Shylock's nose in the mixed marriage of his daughter to Lorenzo that he hates and despises. And furthermore, this moment of depressive feelings and guilt, if that is what it is, does not last for long. Antonio's jealousy nudges Bassanio to give away the ring with which he has married Portia—albeit to a knowing, mischievous Portia (still dressed as a man). But transient though Antonio's depressive feelings may be, it is a reparative act with a beneficial consequence. It affects the relationship between Lorenzo and Jessica, their place in the world, maybe more.

I remember Trevor Nunn's direction of the end of the last scene of the play; the couple with their suitcase—or was it two?—setting out, and the children to come of mixed heritage, journeying to an uncertain future—a future in which the horror and terror of the Holocaust is the defining example of the 20th century of connection and its catastrophic loss. As a member of the audience that night, I feel that Nunn's direction of Shakespeare's play brings home how a reparative, depressive moment is a tiny flame not to be snuffed out.

A COMMON PURPOSE

On an April morning in 2013, I am filled with feelings of awe standing in front of a mysterious object in the British Museum, a mammoth ivory sculpture, 30 cm tall with a lion head and upright male human body, created by a person some 40,000 years ago. *The Lion Man* was part of a small, but stupendous show, *Ice Age Art: Arrival of the Modern Mind* (1). The object has been reconstructed from ivory tusk fragments discovered in the Lone Valley in southwest Germany. Over 200 fragments were discovered in 1939, just before the war. It was another 30 years before the fragments were seen to fit together to form a standing figure, and in 1989 the discovery and restoration of further fragments of the head showed the figure to be a lion— except that it is not a lion. The ideas it communicated way back, in the context of its meanings, and social and symbolic functions, are unknown, but it is a new concept, a new thing.

There is good evidence that the first primitive cells, from which we animals and such creativity evolved, arose four billion years ago, when the earth was just five hundred million years old, part of a solar system when all the planets were being bombarded by chaotic asteroids and bits of rock amid all the forces of the universe (2).

The electromagnetic field, from the earth's rotating core of liquid iron and nickel, protects our *world*. The materials scientist Mark Miodownik, *Start the Week*, BBC Radio 4, 24th December, 2018, says:

We are floating on rock which is so hot that it behaves like a liquid—and below that is a liquid core, iron and nickel, right at the centre of our planet, about 5000 km wide. It is rotating and gives us a magnetic field, and if it weren't for that magnetic field we would be in really bad trouble. We are rained down on by cosmic rays from the sun and other places, and if they were not bounced off or deflected from us, we would quite quickly all be obliterated by the sheer energy, and it would cause mutations, and could kill off probably most of life, and get rid of all the oxygen. We think that is what happened to Mars. When its magnetic field stopped working, it became a desert planet—a dead planet. We are not a dead planet, and that's because we have this liquid core, we are dynamic, we are not a third rock from the sun, we are a third dynamic.

When we see the Northern Lights, created by the destructive power of solar wind hitting the magnetic field, what we are witnessing is how the earth's magnetic field prevents the loss of its atmosphere, without which complex life would not have evolved.

However, around 1.5-2 billion years ago, life on earth was in a period of extended stasis. For two billion years, life had been stuck at the level of two microbial groups—the group of one-cell bacteria and the group of archaea, known as prokaryotes, meaning literally before the nucleus. Then, something happened to structure and link matter to enable the evolution of vastly more complex cells—leading to consciousness and later the modern mind.

The question puzzled Nick Lane (3), a biochemist from the department of Genetics, Evolution and Environment at University College London. He describes how he found a clue in the Nobel Prize-winner Peter Mitchell's idea that cells generate biological energy through a mechanism involving the flow of protons across membranes. Lane writes:

I believe that the clue lies in the bizarre mechanism of biological energy generation in cells. This strange mechanism exerts persuasive but little appreciated physical constraints on cells. Essentially all living cells power themselves through the flow of protons (positively charged hydrogen atoms), in what amounts to a kind of electricity—proticity—with protons in place of electrons. The energy we gain from burning food in respiration is used to pump protons across a membrane, forming a reservoir on one side of the membrane. The flow of protons back from this reservoir can be used to power work in the same way as a turbine in a hydroelectric dam. The use of cross-membrane proton gradients to power cells was utterly unanticipated. First proposed in 1961 and developed over the ensuing three decades by one of the most original scientists of the twentieth century, Peter Mitchell, this conception has been called the most counterintuitive idea in biology since Darwin, and the only one that compares with the ideas of Einstein, Heisenberg and Schrödinger in physics. At the level of proteins, we now know how proton power works in detail. We also know that the use of proton gradients is universal across life on earth—proton power is as much an integral part of all life as the universal genetic code. Yet we know next to nothing about how or why this counterintuitive mechanism of energy-harnessing first evolved (p.13).

Following a great deal of work, it seems that many facts and ideas about prokaryotes and eukaryotic cells became intuitively linked in Lane's imagination through their relationship to Peter Mitchell's new idea of cells being powered by cross-membrane proton gradients. Lane's hypothesis, another new concept, is the idea of a rare event in which one bacterium got inside an archaeon, one

146

cell living inside another, and broke the constraints of the proton gradients. Lane writes:

> I want to show you that the origin of life was driven by energy flux, that proton gradients were central to the emergence of cells, and that their use constrained the structure of both bacteria and archaea. I want to demonstrate that these constraints dominated the later evolution of cells, keeping the bacteria and archaea for ever simple in morphology, despite their biochemical virtuosity. I want to prove that a rare event, an endosymbiosis in which one bacterium got inside an archaeon, broke those constraints, enabling the evolution of vastly more complex cells. I want to show you that this was not easy—that the intimate relationship between cells living one inside another explains why morphologically complex organisms only arose once (pp.13-14).

This rare event created a new form of unprecedented change of function and complexity. It is a complex cell structure of chemical and electrical reactions with nucleus and mitochondria from which multicellular creatures evolve.

> .... all plants, animals, fungi, seaweeds, and single-celled 'protists' such as amoeba—descend from that singular ancestor about 1.5-2 billion years ago. This ancestor was recognisably a 'modern' cell, with an exquisite internal

structure and unprecedented molecular dynamism, all driven by sophisticated nanomachines encoded by thousands of new genes that are largely unknown in bacteria (p. 2).

I have been describing a world, a long time ago, where life got stuck, and where life broke through, when one cell got inside to live in another, breaking an energy restraint, to create a new, complex cell structure. But I have also been describing another interaction between what exists in the universe; an event where one thing gets inside other things in a modern mind to create a new idea, to imagine a new thing. That is to say, Peter Mitchell's new concept (that cells are powered by energy generated by cross-membrane proton gradients) got inside other facts and ideas buzzing around in Nick Lane's mind to break a restraint in how he, Nick Lane, sees the world.

In *The Hidden Spring*, the psychoanalyst Mark Solms (4) describes the experience of the goodness of light as fundamental to the matrix from which consciousness arose.

The ultimate explanation for sentience is a puzzle so difficult it is nowadays referred to reverentially as 'the hard problem'.....

...I imagine the dawn of life in one of those hydro-thermal vents. The unicellular organisms that came into being there would surely not have been conscious, but their survival prospects would have been affected by their ambient surrounds. It is easy to imagine these simple organisms responding to the biological 'goodness' of the energy of the sun. From there, it is a small step to imagine more complex creatures actively striving for such energy supplies and eventually evolving a capacity to weigh the chances of success by alternative actions.

Consciousness, in my view, arose from the experience of such organisms. Picture the heat of the day and cold of the night from the perspective of those first living beings. The physiological values registering their diurnal experiences were the precursors of the first sunrise.

Many philosophers and scientists still believe that sentience serves no physical purpose. My purpose in this book is to persuade you of the plausibility of an alternative interpretation. This requires me to convince you that feelings are part of nature, that they are not fundamentally different from other natural phenomena, and that they *do* something within the causal matrix of things (pp.2-4).

The neuroscientist Gerald Edelman (5) contends that higher order discrimination—that enables us to become aware of our consciousness and to reflect on our experiences—is marked by a way of looking characterised by complexity and integration as well as differentiation. In Edelman's view, human beings recognise patterns in the face of ambiguity of meaning in ways entirely different from computer pattern-recognition experiments.

> ...being selectional systems, [human] brains operate prima facie not by logic but rather by pattern recognition. This process is not precise, as is logic and mathematics. Instead, it trades off specificity and precision, if necessary, to increase its range. It is likely, for example, that early human thought proceeded by metaphor, which, even with the late acquisition of precise means such as logic and mathematical thought, continues to be a major source of imagination and creativity in adult life (p. 58).

Edelman's reference to thoughts first arising before language develops, proceeding by metaphor, and remaining as a major source of imagination and creativity, draws upon the work on "conceptual metaphor" by linguist George Lakoff and philosopher Mark Johnson (6). Lakoff and Johnson shed further light on how a connecting door works in the modern mind. Their ideas of the structuring and linking function of metaphor are not about metaphor in a linguistic sense. They contend that the fundamental ideas of the human animal are structured by systems of what they term "conceptual metaphor"—grounded, shaped and constrained by embodied experience embedded in social interaction. They argue that metaphorical thought is ubiquitous in our mental life, mostly unconscious, with a central role in abstract thought; that metaphors are fundamentally conceptual in nature, and that metaphorical language is secondary.

Lakoff and Johnson see the heart of conceptual metaphor as inference; that we systematically see patterns between one conceptual domain and another conceptual domain, that they call structural metaphors. The correspondence across conceptual domains is what they call metaphorical mapping. We humans are very good at creating analogical patterns between these systems of conceptual metaphor, or as the psychoanalyst Ronald Britton calls them "models in the mind".

The psychoanalyst David Tuckett (7) writes:

> Models of the brain without feelings, for instance as an information-processing device much like a computer, although widespread, miss what is central to human social action... Put simply, algorithms can only treat the future as the past, perhaps adding random variations. Humans... face no such restriction. They develop imaginaries and can *feel* sufficiently convinced by them to try to implement them.

However, a model in the mind might become a delusion. Henri Poincaré (8), the French theoretical physicist, philosopher of science, and mathematician, has an idea of how the unconscious mind plays a necessary part in how an unexpected idea, possibly a new concept—

perhaps after sleeping or out walking, say, or out of the blue—is created—or to put it in another way, how a connecting door works in the modern mind. His idea is a psychological model for how—when a mathematician or scientist is puzzled and frustrated by the inadequacy of existing concepts to explain something and investigates it—a solution to a mathematical or scientific problem may be arrived at.

Poincaré describes his hypothesis in three stages. First, the mathematician or scientist, mulling over a problem puzzling him or her, consciously *selects* a number of facts and ideas. This stage might happen over a long period of time. Poincaré uses the term "select" to emphasise that the ideas and facts selected are *not* random but those seen by the thinker as relevant. The selected facts are aspects of the thinker's knowledge selected *by the will*.

In the second stage of the model, the thinker's *informed intuition* leads to an interaction where other accumulated past and current facts and ideas may unconsciously fall into a new pattern, that may be a new concept, by their relationship to one or more of the selected facts.

Poincaré sees the unconscious mind (searching for a pattern that would be a solution to the problem being investigated) as capable of forming in a brief space of time more *combinations* than could be done consciously in a whole lifetime—a number of combinations that, as he puts it, "staggers the imagination". (It seems highly likely that this aspect of the hypothesis Poincaré put forward more than 100 years ago involves energy transfer at the quantum level, which I will come to below.)

Poincaré argues that only those combinations emerge from the unconscious mind into consciousness "which, directly or indirectly, most deeply affect our sensibility." As he also puts it, these are combinations "which are capable of developing in us a kind of aesthetic emotion… those [combinations] whose elements are harmoniously arranged so that the mind can, without effort, take in the whole without neglecting the details."

However, Poincaré also contends that that these unconscious processes through which such combinations emerge are necessary but not sufficient. A construction we imagine, an emerging idea, that we feel sufficiently convinced by that we seek to implement it, may be a delusional belief. Emergence of a combination into consciousness carries a sense of conviction, but he argues, "all we can hope for from these inspirations, which are fruits of unconscious work, is to obtain points of departure… (p. 62)."

Poincaré's warning echoes the tale of a boy from Birmingham; his experience of a religious conversion, a combination emerging from unconscious processes, that is a counter-belief system—covering up an underlying, unconscious, catastrophic belief. Poincaré argues that his model of discovery has a third stage, dispassionate observation—investigation, evaluation and testing of the combination that emerges into consciousness.

In the late-'80s, the electrochemist Martin Fleischmann, whose family moved to England from Czechoslovakia before the war to escape the tyranny of Nazi persecution, who was my tutor as a chemistry undergraduate at Newcastle-upon-Tyne—published research that he and his collaborator Stanley Pons believed demonstrated heat production from a low energy nuclear reaction, "cold fusion". Replication—an analogical process where different people in different places carry out the reported experiment to see whether the findings are similar—is a key instrument of evaluation in scientific experimentation. If reliably replicated, a potential source of clean energy suggested by Fleischmann's published observation would have been promising. But colleagues had difficulty replicating the findings, which remain controversial.

Was the difficulty in replication a consequence of a premature integration of experimental observation and theory? Was an internal tyrant quietly at work? If sufficient time, effort and money had been poured into further attempts at replication, the question about cold fusion could have been settled definitively. However, we may never know. The money has followed not cold fusion but hot fusion as a source of clean energy, with considerable financial, scientific and commercial investment.

Civilisation depends upon informed intuition and inference, needing testing and evaluation, to find solutions to new problems that change always brings. Poincaré's model of a psychological *pathway* is a guide to how a connecting door works in the modern mind. How one thing getting inside another to produce a combination *may* be a solution to a problem, may be a new thing. But it may, without appropriate evaluation, be a crystallisation of a delusional conviction. A limited and limiting world, where reality forces us to relinquish possession of the source of goodness, of light, may be invaded and occupied by an internal tyrant.

As children, we make a relationship with what exists through the relationship with our parents, or other carers, and continue our explorations through other mediums— history, literature, law, politics, painting, economics, philosophy, music, theatre, film, dance, poetry, theology, design, construction, sculpture, physics, chemistry, mathematics, neuroscience, geography, astronomy, anthropology, palaeontology, aeronautics, medicine, psychology, engineering, architecture, sociology, and so on. Disciplines can become rigid but at best are informed by ideals that are open and supported by international communities of workers across generations and borders. And this is very far from being a newly minted, modern phenomenon as Seb Falk (9) tells us in his enlightening account of the story of medieval science centring on the almost unknown figure of 14th century Benedictine monk John of Westwick. Like now, science developed through the industry of talented individuals and was international.

A part of the task of the disciplines is the evaluation of ideas that may be crystallisations of a delusional conviction. Cross-discipline investigation may play an important part in the task. Leach's idea of the post-exilic myth is an example of how an idea from one discipline, getting inside ideas from another discipline, can change our way of seeing.

New combinations may emerge from an existing vision and be of immense value, making people's lives better. For example, Alexander Fleming's discovery of penicillin, an antibacterial agent, was an on-going battle with bacterial infection—following injuries in the First World War. Fleming's discovery of penicillin was almost accidental, but his work led to the antibiotic revolution that changed lives and expectations. If Fleming's discovery of penicillin (on the morning of Friday 28th September, 1928) had happened at an earlier time, my three-year-old dad's 42-year-old father would very probably not have died from pneumonia.

However, from time to time a new thing emerges through a connecting door that profoundly changes how we look at *our* world. We see it in the emergence of the Renaissance. Stephen Greenblatt (10) describes this in *The Swerve*, a book named after Lucretius' ideas in the poem *On the Nature of Things*, written more than two thousand years ago. In scientific inquiry, Thomas Kuhn, in *The Structure of Scientific Revolutions* (11), calls this kind of phenomenon a paradigm change. It can generate great controversy around the relationship between old and new, as is true of quantum mechanics, the most remarkable new concept to emerge from the sciences in the twentieth century. It is a hypothetical mathematical model, created by Max Planck and Niels Bohr and their colleagues, that is beyond the comprehension of most people, certainly including myself, other than by analogy.

Jim Al-Khalili of the University of Surrey—in two television programmes, *The Secrets of Quantum Mechanics*, BBC Four, December 2014—gives a picture of quantum theory using analogical models. He describes how a key step in the conception of quantum physics— as Mitchell's new notion of proton gradients was crucial in Nick Lane's new concept—was a new thing getting into other things. The new thing in this case was Albert Einstein's discovery of the new concept of light as carrying variable amounts of energy—a lot of energy at the blue and ultra-violet end of the light spectrum and much less energy at the red end. It was this new thing, Einstein's discovery of a new concept about the nature of light, getting into the minds of Max Planck and Niels Bohr, which led by the late 1920s to the creation of the new theory of quantum mechanics that describes the world of the very small.

The conception of this new idea of the nature of light in Einstein's mind was itself a solution to a theoretical puzzle of the inadequacy of the concepts of classical Newtonian physics to comprehend reality as demonstrated by new scientific observations. In Newtonian physics the nature of light is taken as a given; light is a wave of energy. An example of these new observations was the unexplained connection between light and electricity, which became known as the "photo-electric effect". This effect can be reliably demonstrated with a gold leaf electroscope—a horizontal electrical conducting metal surface from which is suspended two gold leaves hinged together, as indeed I remember being demonstrated in a science lesson at school. If the electroscope is charged up with static electricity, the electrical charge (extra electrons) pushes the conducting hinged gold leaves apart. That is the "base-line". Now if we take red light and shine it on the metal surface, nothing happens, even if we increase the brightness of the red light. The two gold leaves are not affected. But if we shine blue light, which is rich in ultra-violet light, onto the metal plate, the two hinged gold leaves collapse together into a vertical position. Blue light, unlike red light, can clearly remove the static electrical charge, somehow knocking out the electrons added by the charge.

This phenomenon is not explained in the classical Newtonian model, where the nature of light is a wave of energy, taken, as I say, as a given. The new idea born in

Einstein's mind that light carries variable amounts of energy was able to predict scientific observations that could not be comprehended through the classical model of light. It was for this explanation of the "photo-electric effect", in a paper in 1905, that Einstein won the Nobel Prize.

It is part of the genius of Einstein's mind to bear sufficiently with the disturbance of un-synthesised reality that he was able to question a given—the importance of which is not restricted to the sciences. I remember a Royal Academy exhibition art critic's comment that necessary for the birth of the new is a mind with the capacity to *allow the memory of things and the facts as they appear to be filtered by imagination.*

It was repeatedly replicated experimentally that, in the quantum world, individual sub-atomic particles, like the electron and proton, or quanta of light (the photon), can behave like a wave.

The laws of quantum mechanics are common sense-defying. The spread-out, fuzzy, wave-like behaviour of sub-atomic particles enables them to leap though an energy barrier, to tunnel, appearing and disappearing fleetingly. However, the receptivity of chemistry and biology to these foreign ideas of quantum mechanics—one thing getting into another thing to create a new idea—has led to some amazing discoveries. It appears that the underlying quantum nature of reality underpins and shapes the living world. Uncertainty is part and parcel of the mechanisms that capture energy from the sun, on which all life depends. Al-Khalili describes Alexandra Olaya-Castro's (University College London) discovery of how quantum mechanics changes our understanding of the first stage of photosynthesis, the process in the leaves of green plants in which the light of the sun, water, and carbon dioxide generate oxygen and glucose. It has long been the stuff of school biology textbooks that in the first stage of photosynthesis a photon from the sun knocks an electron out of the middle of a chlorophyll molecule to create a packet of energy. But sixty years ago, when I answered a question on this in my biology "O" level paper, the mechanism by which a packet of energy can reach the reaction centre of the living cell so fast that photosynthesis is almost 100% efficient—far and away more efficient than any machine-made energy transfer—was an unsolved puzzle. Al-Khalili conveys the awe he feels about the new story of energy transfer that emerged from Olaya-Castro's imagination:

> The packet of energy is heading in every direction at the same time, spreading itself out as a wave, so it can explore all possible routes simultaneously. The packet of energy is not just going this way or that way. It is following all paths at the same time. That is what gives it such incredible efficiency. The beauty of it is that as the energy packet is trying every

route at once, it is bound to find the fastest possible way to deliver its energy. It is hard to express how incredible this discovery seems to a physicist like me. Biological cells are full of the random juggling of atoms and molecules but somehow the energy packets retain their form as beautiful quantum waves, transporting the energy that guarantees life on earth.

There is, at least thus far, no single narrative giving meaning to the mathematical equations of quantum theory, but it brings new scientific understanding and advances that have made our lives better. To take one example, my mother lived for some thirty years after my father died with what she called her "cloth ears". It is likely that her hearing loss was similar to a high-frequency hearing loss that I was diagnosed with when I was 60. Without a modern digital hearing aid, the work and effort involved in conversation would have become so stressful, that I would not have been able to continue to work as a psychoanalyst.

At a recent hearing test, I felt disturbed and vulnerable to find how hard I have to work (without my hearing aid) to comprehend and repeat even a few words from recorded sentences of unfamiliar voices, especially with a slight accent. I had lost a little bit more of my capacity to process high frequency sounds, essential to making sense of speech. This deterioration could be corrected with a new hearing aid model. I was amazed to discover how much the technology had developed over just a few years.

The first digital hearing aid was commercialised around 1996, only five years before my mother's death—too late to help her. The experience of my last hearing test made me a lot more empathic to the vulnerability and anxiety that her loss of hearing brought to her.

Poincaré's psychological model, where we may discover solutions to a problem, starts with our curiosity. We select *by the will*, through informed intuition, and selection of facts and ideas we see as relevant. This leads to interaction with accumulated past and current facts, and ideas may unconsciously fall into a new pattern, maybe a new concept, by their relationship to one or more of the selected facts.

But, as I have described, there is another aspect of this model, implicitly recognised by Poincaré in his attention to evaluation. It is the necessity to mourn what fails appropriate tests of evaluation, to avoid delusion. I think Sigmund Freud's model of mourning is integral to Poincaré's model. Mourning something is the upending of the way we know and relate to a person, a belief or a situation. What we mourn is a relationship to something that has its own life but which in our subjective experience (to a certain extent) remains a concrete possession; something which reality now insists *against the will* is lost and gone for ever in each and every part of life where it had a place. Freud describes how this painful process allows us to internalise a relationship the person, belief or situation symbolically as part of us—freeing us to be able to relate to something new. But, even though mourning has its natural path, remembrance and sadness for what is lost and gone for ever is never fully done with.

Let me end by describing the making of art through four different houses—an old people's home, a curved building, a royal house, and a house created in autumn 1993, and demolished on 11th January, 1994.

OLD PEOPLES HOME (2010)

CURVED BUILDING (2015)

The potter Alice Mara, mourning the death of her mother, that followed the early death of her printmaker father, produced several series of ceramic funeral urns using a complex photographic technique. In *Old Peoples Home,* we see young people getting on with living their lives, walking past *Home* along a pleasant suburban street, while through the semi-translucent blinds of *Home*, is another "young person", the artist, working with her feelings of loss, missing, anger, love, hate, longing, guilt.

Alice Mara's funeral urn series reaches its end five years later in a "slab-built" piece, *Curved Building*. The potter's mourning for what is lost and gone forever leads to the release of more life. Protruding above colourful old shops, a home—or homes—of curving fertility bursts outwards; the burgeoning of shape and crackle glaze is alarming. On the side of the home a "young person" is falling, hands gripping a ledge. The loss and mourning of a loved person, belief or situation, with finding of a new thing, is never free of an internal tyrant that seeks to invade.

Of course, I cannot know what Alice Mara was thinking. This is what I imagine as I look at these pots.

At the time the art critic Laura Cummings (12) was mourning her father, in the Prado on a hunt for El Greco, one of her father's favourite painters, she passed the opening to a large gallery, when a strange frisson of light caught the edge of her eye.

"As I turned to look, all the people standing at the other end of the gallery suddenly moved aside as one, clearing an open view to the source of that light; Velázquez's monumental *Las Meninas*. I had no thought of it, no idea it would be there or how vast it would be—an image the size of life, and fully as profound... The moment you set eyes on them, you know that these beautiful children will die, that they are already dead and gone, and yet they live in the here and now, of this moment, brief and bright, as fireflies beneath the sepulchral gloom. And what keeps them here, what keeps them alive, or so the artist implies is not just the painting but you...

But take a few steps towards the painting in all its astounding veracity and the vision swithers. The princess's lustrous hair begins to look like a mirage, or a heatwave scintillating above a summer road that vanishes at your approach. The face of the lady dwarf dissolves into illegible brushstrokes. The figures in the background become inchoate at point-blank range and you can no longer see where a hand stops and the tray it is holding begins. The nearer you get to the painting, the more these semblances of reality start to disappear, to the point where it is impossible to fathom how the image could have been made in the first place. Everything is on the verge of dissolution and yet so vividly present that the sunshine in the painting seems to float free and drift out

into the gallery. It is the most spellbinding vision in art."
(pp. 1-3)

I see *Las Meninas* (Diego Velázquez c. 1656) on a visit to Madrid at Easter 2001. Velázquez incorporates the beautiful children, the Infanta Margarita, and two maids of honour, the two dwarfs, the dog, Philip IV, Hapsburg king of a world power in decline—the Eighty Years' War of revolt by the Netherlands against Catholic rule had recently ended with the establishment of the Protestant Dutch Republic—and his second wife, Queen Maria Anna, other figures, doors, windows, mirrors, and a reflection of himself at work with brush and palette on the vast canvas.

Velázquez invites the seer to move in and out, to look and to look away, to identify and dis-identify, over whatever timescale, to imagine and reflect through whatever medium.

In much contemporary thought, vision is demonized as perforce a gaze of subjective command over an object which appropriates the seen in terms of the projections of the seer, which reduces the object to an inert stoniness. This critique ignores the way in which it is the particular which can hold one's gaze not in a mode of abjection, but through the lure of fascination before the inexhaustibly specific.
Catherine Pickstock. Norris-Hulse Professor of Divinity, University of Cambridge, (13).

Anthony Whishaw, a Royal Academician early in his career, created many works in the mid-eighties related to Velázquez's *Las Meninas*. He writes:

> The ambiguous spatial possibilities of these openings and their surrounding structures are an arena facilitating one of my main pre-occupations, that of an image in the process of formation, a kind of mental cubism, which holds back just before realisation; that intense moment before perception. The juggling with contradictions, allusions, illusions, visual puns and irony presents a stage—into which the viewer can project—hopefully to conceive a new visual entity that relates back to life, ideas of memory and experience.

Anthony Whishaw "does not do dogs" but something about Baz led him to become a sitter. Baz, like Jim, loves to be out and about; loving the freedom to walk, jump, run, sometimes run off but also the opportunity to sniff. In the need to explore *our* world, Baz's capacity to detect and enjoy smells is as fundamental as Whishaw's capacity to juggle with spatial possibilities. Dogs are capable of detecting and analysing a vastly greater number of smells than us. However, our human capacity to detect smells is more considerable than we might suppose. In *How We Detect Smells, The Life Scientific*, 3rd March, 2020, BBC Radio 4, Al-Khalili interviews the Nobel Prize-winner Matthew Cobb. Al-Khalili begins with the observation that there are a lot of different smells out there; the latest estimates suggest that we humans are capable of detecting more than a trillion different smells.

Baz
Anthony Whishaw

Cobb confirms that there is no sensible limit to what we can detect. Most of Cobb's work on smell has been done on patterns of courtship and mating of fruit flies and larvae. He and his colleagues have shown that the structure of how a sense of smell works in humans, dogs, rats and fruit flies is basically the same. We think that we

170

smell with our nose but actually we smell with our brain. A particular pheromone, some hydrocarbon molecule, floats in and turns a key in a particular receptor, attached to a neurone that sends an electrical signal up to the brain. And here the way we detect a smell gets complex. The signal sent to the brain by the neurone is not an off-on signal. The profile of the signal is not binary; it is an analogue signal.

As Al–Khalili puts it at the end of the interview with Matthew Cobb, we still don't understand how smell works.

But, from an evolutionary point of view, I think a possible inference is that smell, like music, is part of the foundations of systems of conceptual metaphor.

On 5th January, 2018, I make it just in time, not long before the end of Rachel Whiteread's retrospective exhibition at Tate Britain. Laura Cummings says (14): Rachel Whiteread has been turning things inside out for the last thirty years. I watch a video with Whiteread's commentary of *"House"* in Grove Road, Bow that she created in autumn 1993, and which is demolished on 11th January, 1994. I am moved, remembering walking around *"House"* one Saturday that Christmas, and a week or so later seeing it, strange, close to the road as I pass in the car. Whiteread made *"House"* from the last dwelling left standing of a Victorian terrace in East London. Similar terraces in the East End were bombed to pieces in the havoc and destruction of the blitz, or later demolished to make way for tower blocks.

Whiteread says in the video, *we are making a building within a building*; the curtains and other stuff left behind come out, new deeper concrete foundations are laid to hold up the sculpture, then the "filling in" with white-coloured concrete bound by a metal structure, then the brick walls pulled down. 25th October to 11th January, 1994 people from all over the place came to see and to look.

Rachel Whiteread creates a work of art that is a building within a building that touches our feelings, our minds, our hopes. And it stimulates our curiosity: *What is going on*? Making a building within a building is a metaphor for what I am attempting to do in this book. A thing striking me most in Whiteread's video is the night shot—*"House"* lit up, people still looking, walking round it, wanting to get inside, and meeting the insistence of the reality that *"House"* and those who inhabited it over time are lost and gone for ever.

This work, like *"House"* is, I hope, a making of art where the seer is taken to a connecting door, where reality insists he or she cannot cross. And the thing is, we might tumble into discovering more, different, exciting, challenging interconnections in *our world* than we ever imagined.

No such thing as Never Again

And the thing is, we might tumble into a delusion. It is midday on Mothering Sunday in the Wigmore Hall, the 32nd day of the terrible, frightening war in Ukraine, Putin's war. I am sitting at end of the Row E between Claire and Bruce in seats 5, 6 and 7. The Wihan Quartet, a Czech string quartet have played Sergey Taneyev's *String Quartet No. 1* (1890)—a piece by a Russian composer that is new to me. The audience give loud and very warm applause to the players who smile with happiness at the appreciation and the evident sense of solidarity. As they go backstage, I see the back of a man with short black hair leave seat 5 row D and walk forward a few paces to go through the beautiful, tall doors to the left of the stage, marked Emergency Exit, a connecting door to life. The man's exit is a bit of an unusual happening in the brief interval in these Sunday morning concerts.

Half a minute later, my attention moves to the return of the players to play Benjamin Britten's *String Quartet No. 2*, written at the end of the war. As they begin, my attention shifts. I notice a medium-size black haversack that now occupies seat 5 row D. I feel fear. This intimate concert hall is unlikely to rate a high risk on any list of possible targets for a terrorist attack. But what is that worth if there is a murderous intention to make an attack in the centre of London to show the reach of the hand of terror against a demonstration of a common purpose against tyranny? The playing of Britten's quartet continues. My fright grows. Is this the last quartet for me, for Claire, for Bruce, for the quartet, for so many in the hall? I imagine the man with the black hair not far away, the other side of the tall emergency doors, phone in hand, ready to detonate the bomb a yard away that will blow us to atoms and our families into shock and grief. As we are taken into the ending of the quartet, I think *is this the moment he is waiting for, listening, a bomber who is a musician?* The last notes fade. The end. The applause. The man sitting in front in seat 6 row D releases the strap to his black rucksack resting on seat 5, moved for convenience away from his feet after the departure of the man with short black hair.

Ignês Sodré describes the Fall from a psychoanalytic point of view in the dawning of the Oedipus situation. "The ideal object always causes some humiliation at the moment of the first realisation of separateness because as the object is seen more realistically, i.e., no longer as a possession and with the idealisation gone, the Fall is too great... Normally the mother's love saves the day, since it creates a link and is felt to rescue the baby from the abyss." But there is blood on the tracks. Subjective experience of connection and its catastrophic loss—we all have a bit of it—brings an underlying, unconscious, catastrophic belief that we have injured a connecting door to goodness, invasion by an internal tyrant, and an idealised, paranoid counter-belief system of one kind or another.

I illustrate the havoc this brings in the tale of a boy from Birmingham. I further illustrate this kind of phenomenon, with a hypothesis that I call hardened myth in the relationship between Judaism and Christianity down the centuries. Hardened myth is two myths, two paranoid, idealized ideologies, mirroring each other. In the Jewish post-exilic myth, the dispossessed Samaritans are the near foreigner group into which vulnerability and damage are projected with virtuous hatred. In the Christian Jesus myth, the dispossessed Jews are the near foreigner group into which vulnerability and damage are projected with virtuous hatred.

We see similar phenomenon in our world today in the use of the internet and social media, to manipulate dispossessed groups with disinformation to spread delusional perceptions and ideologies to gain power, with an aim of disrupting and destroying a whole way of life. The spread of disinformation contributes to the havoc of manmade climate change, and loss of ecosystems.

The world of an internal tyrant promises permanent well-being, and demands propitiation for loss, for vulnerability, for fallibility, and for mistakes, errors and wrongdoing. We split off, and project its horrors into another or others—creating havoc. Very different is a world where we feel guilt and sorrow, where we mourn what is lost and gone forever, and where we work to do all we can to make things better, inasmuch as reality allows. However, the two different worlds are close in our minds. An internal tyrant, with its specious authority, is always on the watch for opportunities to invade and occupy the vulnerable, imperfect world of a third position. *Norr Saws* and *The Adoration of the Kings in the Snow* show us *our* world in the here and now. It is why we need to keep on asking questions and being asked questions.

Creativity or tyranny—from that warfare there is no release (1).

Endnotes

Introduction

1. His Holiness, The Dalai Lama with Franz Alt. *Our Only Home*, 2019, p. 51. London: Daunt Books.
2. Seamus Heaney. *New Selected Poems. 1988-2013.* 2014, London: Faber & Faber.

Minding the shop

1. After Jessy Mair. *See* Peter Hennessy, *Never Again,* p.73 Peter Hennessy, *Never Again,* Britain 1945-1951. 1992, London: Jonathan Cape, pp. 72-74.

It's upsetting to see your mother cry

1. William Shakespeare. *The Winter's Tale*. Ed. Ernest Schanzer. 1969, London: Penguin.

2. Rob Sheldon, conservationist. Talk to the "London Bird Club", Highgate, 12th November, 2019.

3. Gillian Clarke. Selected Poems. 2016, London: Picador.

4. *Lectures on Technique by Melanie Klein.* Edited with critical Review by John Steiner. 2017, Abingdon, Oxon: Routledge p. 37.

5. Ronald Britton, 'The Triangular Model'. In: Ronald Britton. *Between Mind and Brain: Models of the Mind and Models in the Mind.* 2015, London: Karnac.

6. Dana Birksted-Breen. Phallus, penis and mental space. *The International Journal of Psychoanalysis,* 1996. Volume 77, pp. 649-657.

7. *Pappano's Classical Voices: Mezzo-Soprano* BBC4 12th July, 2015.

8. John Bridcut. *Janet Baker in Her Own Words.* BBC4 14th April, 2019.

A HIGGLEDY-PIGGLEDY FALL

1. John Cox. *Elizabeth, The Forgotten Years.* 2016. London: Viking

2. Neil MacGregor. *Germany. Memories of a Nation.* 2014 London: Allen Lane.

3. *You say you want a Revolution. Records and Rebels 1966-1970.* 2016, London: V&A.

GOING NORTH

1. Horace Edwin Hayden. Pub 1891. *GLASSELL of Scotland and Virginia. Virginia Genealogies. A Genealogy of THE GLASSELL FAMILY.*
2. Herbert S Klein. *The Atlantic Slave Trade.* 2010, Cambridge: Cambridge University Press p. 44.
3. David McKenzie Robertson. *From Roucan to Riches. The Rise of the Glassell Family.* 2020, Kibworth Beauchamp: Matador.
4. T M Devine. *The Scottish Clearances: A History of the Dispossessed 1600-1900.* 2018, UK: Allen Lane.

BORN OF DAVID'S LINE

1. Joseph Leo Koerner. Professor of the History of Art and Architecture at Harvard University. Joseph Leo Koerner. *Bosch and Bruegel: From Enemy Painting to Everyday Life.* 2016, Princeton and Oxford: Princeton University Press.

2. John Bowker. Prophets, Priests, and Kings: The Transformation. In: *The Religious Imagination and the Sense of God.* 1978, Oxford: OUP pp. 77-96.
3. Robert Alter. *The David Story.* 1999, New York, London: Norton pp. xviii-xix.
4. *I Am Ashurbanipal: King of the World, King of Assyria. 2018.* Ed Gareth Brereton. Thames & Hudson in collaboration with the British Museum: UK.
5. Edmund Leach. *Genesis as Myth and Other Essays.* 1969, London: Jonathan Cape.
6. Henri Poincaré. *Science and Method* (2007). New York: Cosimo Classics. First published in 1908, and translated in this edition by Francis Maitland in 1914. Chapter III, Mathematical Discovery.
7. David Millar. A Psychoanalytical View of Biblical Myth. *International Journal of Psychoanalysis,* 2001. Volume 82, pp. 965-979.
8. Charles Freeman. *AD 381: Heretics, Pagans, and the Christian State.* 2009, London: Pimlico.
9. John Bowker. The Religious Imagination and the Sense of God. In: *The Religious Imagination and the Sense of God,* 1978, Oxford: OUP pp. 306—318.
10. David Nirenberg. In Orange-Tawny Bonnets. *London Review of Books.* Volume 40, Number 3, 8th February, 2018, pp. 19-21

11. William Shakespeare. *The Merchant of Venice*. Ed W. Moelwyn Merchant. 1967, London: Penguin.

A COMMON PURPOSE

1. Jill Cook. *Ice Age Art: Arrival of the Modern Mind* 2013. British Museum.
2. The research astrophysicist Carole Haswell, *Start the Week*, BBC Radio 4, 21st December, 2015.
3. Nick Lane. *The Vital Question: Why Is Life the Way It Is?* 2015, London: Profile Books.
4. Mark Solms. *The Hidden Spring. A Journey to the Source of Consciousness*. 2021, London: Profile Books.
5. Gerald Edelman. *Second Nature, Brain Science and Human Knowledge*. 2006, Yale: New Haven.
6. George Lakoff and Mark Johnson. *Metaphors We Live By (1980) Afterword (2003),* pp. 243 -274.
7. David Tuckett. 'Feeling, Narrative and Mental States: How neuroeconomics can shift the Paradigm'. In: Kirman, A. and Teschi, M. *The State of Mind in Economics.* In press, Cambridge University Press.
8. Henri Poincaré. *Science and Method.* 2007, New York: Cosimo Classics. First published in 1908, and translated in this edition by Francis Maitland in 1914. Chapter III, Mathematical Discovery.

9. Seb Falk. *The Light Ages: A Medieval Journey of Discovery.* 2020, UK: Allen Lane.

10. Stephen Greenblatt. *The Swerve: How the World Became Modern.* 2011, W.W. Norton: New York & London.

11. Thomas Kuhn. *The Structure of Scientific Revolutions* (1962) with an introductory essay by Ian Hacking. 2012, Chicago and London: The University of Chicago Press.

12. Laura Cummings. *The Vanishing Man: In Pursuit of Velázquez* 2016. London: Chatto & Windus. pp.1-3.

13. Catherine Pickstock. Faculty of Divinity Newsletter. Theology, Religion, & Philosophy of Religion. Issue 3, January 2019.

14. Laura Cummings, Review of Rachel Whiteread's retrospective Exhibition at Tate Britain. The Observer, New Review, pp. 24-25, *Observer*, 17th September, 2017.

NO SUCH THING AS NEVER AGAIN

1. After W. R. Bion—with thanks to Simona Di Segni.

www.ingramcontent.com/pod-product-compliance
Lightning Source LLC
Chambersburg PA
CBHW051517120626
46551CB00012B/970